A
Persistent
Voice

A Persistent Voice

Marian Franz
*and Conscientious
Objection to
Military Taxation*

Edited by
David R. Bassett,
Steve Ratzlaff & Tim Godshall

Foreword by
Andy Jacobs

Cascadia

Publishing House
Telford, Pennsylvania

copublished with
Peace Tax Foundation
Washington, D.C. *and*

Herald Press
Scottdale, Pennsylvania

Cascadia Publishing House orders, information, reprint permissions:
contact@CascadiaPublishingHouse.com
1-215-723-9125
126 Klingerman Road, Telford PA 18969
www.CascadiaPublishingHouse.com

A Persistent Voice

Published by Cascadia Publishing House, a division of
Cascadia Publishing House LLC, Telford, PA 18969
Copublished with Herald Press, Scottdale, PA
Library of Congress Catalog Number: 2008054888
ISBN-13: 978-1-931038-59-1; **ISBN 10:** 1-931038-59-7
Book and cover design and back cover photo by Tim Godshall; front cover
photo of Marian Franz during the 1992 House Ways and Means Committee
Hearing by John Eisele; photo of Capitol courtesy Deamstime Photos.

The paper used in this publication is recycled and meets the
minimum requirements of American National Standard for Information Sciences—Permanence of Paper for Printed Library Materials, ANSI Z39.48-1984.

All Bible quotations used by permission, all rights reserved and, unless otherwise
noted, are from *The New Revised Standard Version of the Bible*, copyright 1989, by
the Division of Christian Education of the National Council of the Churches of
Christ in the USA.

Library of Congress Cataloguing-in-Publication Data
Franz, Marian C. (Marian Claassen), 1930-2006.
  A persistent voice : Marian Franz and conscientious objection to military taxation / edited by David R. Bassett, Steve Ratzlaff, and Tim Godshall ; fore-
word by Andy Jacobs.
    p. cm.
  Summary: "These essays by Marian Franz span her 23 years of lobbying
Congress to enact the Peace Tax Fund Bill, which would allow conscientious
objectors to pay taxes into a fund for nonmilitary purposes only. Franz is
joined by eight colleagues who contribute chapters unique to their perspec-
tives and expertise on related topics." "[summary]"--Provided by publisher.
  ISBN-13: 978-1-931038-59-1 (6 x 9" trade pbk. : alk. paper)
  ISBN-10: 1-931038-59-7 (6 x 9" trade pbk. : alk. paper)
  1. War tax resistance--United States. 2. Conscientious objectors--United
States. I. Bassett, David R., 1928- II. Ratzlaff, Steve, 1945- III. Godshall, Tim.
IV. Title.

HJ4653.E75F73 2009
336.2--dc22

                                    2008054888

        16 15 14 13 12 11 10 09   10 9 8 7 6 5 4 3 2 1

Contents

PART II A Persistent Voice: Selected Essays by Marian Franz

Editor's Preface

I came to know Marian Franz during the last three years of her twenty-three-year tenure as executive director at the National Campaign for a Peace Tax Fund (NCPTF). Soon after I began my job as NCPTF's outreach and development director, Marian shared with me her list of projects she wished to complete before, or shortly after, she retired. One of the items on this long list was to compile for publication her twenty-three years' worth of newsletter columns.

Marian's column was a regular feature in the Peace Tax Fund Newsletter, which came out three or four times a year. How do you write about the same issue for over two decades without running out of fresh insights? Marian had that ability. With stories gleaned from lobbying visits, extensive reading, travels, and life experience, Marian consistently crafted essays full of hope and inspiration that, while centered on the legislative effort to enact the Peace Tax Fund Bill, touched on a broad array of themes. For good reason, many readers found Marian's column to be the highlight of the Peace Tax Fund Newsletter.

As is often the case in a small non-profit, urgent day-to-day matters crowd out the longer-term projects. This compilation of essays was no exception to that trend. I recall Marian's last NCPTF board meeting before she retired, in preparation for which she photocopied a political cartoon on the final page of the agenda. The cartoon, by Jeff Danziger, was from early July 2005, just after Supreme Court Justice Sandra Day O'Connor announced her retirement. It portrays a white-haired woman in a black robe, leaping from a swing with arms outstretched, into mid-air. This, Marian explained to us, is how she was viewing her own retirement. Looking at that cartoon, it was not hard to imagine Marian in that position, leaping into the air, embracing the unknown. As it turned out, the unknown awaiting her would be the recurrence of cancer that would take her life only a year later.

Needless to say, many of Marian's hopes for her retirement—part-time lobbying, easing the transition to a new NCPTF director, and working on the book of columns—took a back seat to the immediate task of dealing with her illness. Even as she suffered, Marian seemed to approach the indignities of her disease with the same curiosity and compassion that marked her life in the political world.

About a year after her November 17, 2006, death, NCPTF board members Steve Ratzlaff and David Bassett joined me in deciding to bring this project to completion. This book is the result of those efforts. We have selected, out of over seventy columns, forty-seven which represent the scope of Marian's writings. These are printed in chronological order in Part II of the book.

We also have contacted a number of Marian's colleagues to write chapters on their respective areas of expertise. This additional content appears in Part I of the book, as a way to familiarize readers with the context in which Marian's work took place. These chapters also outline the issues facing those who continue the work of promoting Peace Tax Fund legislation. We are grateful to these authors—Andy Jacobs, Barbara Green, L. William Yolton, Ruth Benn, Edward F. Snyder, Derek Brett and Willard M. Swartley—for their profound contributions to this book.

We would like to thank the staff of NCPTF for their support along the way, particularly intern Emily Stutzman for her long hours typing hard copies of old newsletter columns into the computer. We are grateful for the willingness of Cascadia Publishing House to copublish this book with the Peace Tax Foundation, and for the invaluable help from Cascadia's Michael A. King in the publication process. And of course, we are most grateful for Marian Franz and the persistent, prophetic voice with which she speaks so clearly in the pages to come. We believe that you will be challenged and inspired by her message, as so many have been.

—Tim Godshall

Foreword

As I think about the life and work of Marian Franz and read her essays published here, two movies come to mind: Jessamyn West's *Friendly Persuasion*, in which the Hoosier Quaker who declines to go to war is told by his combatant, non-Quaker friend, "It's good to see someone holding out for a better way of settling things," and Han Suyin's *Love is a Many-Splendored Thing*, in which the heroine says, "there is nothing stronger in the world than gentleness."

Another phrase that Marian considered important was "Blessed are the peacemakers." Therefore, many times blessed was our many-splendored friend and blazing talent Marian Franz. In her pleasant and lovely way, she uttered gentle and powerful words for a better way of handling federal income tax obligations of conscientious objectors whose consciences will not allow them to help finance military activities. One way is to send them to prison. The better way? The same way the government handles such citizens in the case of military service, where conscientious objectors are enabled to perform non-combatant or alternative civilian service.

Conscientious objector status is as old as our republic. The first president to support governmental accommodation of conscientious objection was—the first president. At the start of the Revolutionary War, George Washington issued a call for "all young men of suitable age to be drafted, except those with conscientious scruples against war."

The better way than prison, in the case of federal taxes, is to allow conscientious objectors to pay their full amount of taxes for any government purpose but military. The effect of the Peace Tax Fund Bill, when enacted by Congress, will be to provide for "alternative service for tax dollars." There are plenty of government expenditures besides military, and the Peace Tax Fund would not reduce U.S. government spending on the military by one cent. Considering the amount of junk the Pentagon buys at jewelry prices, such spending should be reduced, but the Peace Tax Fund would have nothing to do with that reform.

The beginning of my involvement with the Religious Freedom Peace Tax Fund Bill started with a phone call to our Tenth District Indiana Congressional Office in Washington. "My name is Marian Franz. May I speak to your administrative assistant?" My coworker David Wildes took the call, an appointment followed, and thus began a beautiful friendship between Marian and David. Once Marian explained her Peace Tax Fund mission, David suggested a meeting with the congressman, who happened to be myself. There would be very many more such encounters. Marian knew that during her long and tiring day she was more than welcome to relax in our office, to make herself at home. And whenever she did, a special sparkle arrived with her.

She was modest, quiet, brilliant, and beautiful to the heart, to the soul and to the eye. Marian was eloquent, polite, typically soft-spoken—and persuasive. It was a privilege to work with her on the legislation of which I became a sponsor, along with the magnificent Senator Mark Hatfield of Oregon. We were granted a hearing before a House Ways and Means Subcommittee. The case for the Peace Tax Fund Bill was made beyond any logical debate to the contrary, but there was an obstacle. Many politicians perceive a peculiarity among the American public that sees violence as an index to patriotism. And in many cases that index overrides reason. It is the task of "blessed peacemakers" to dispel such superficial logic.

It has been said that politics is the art of the possible. It has also been said that statesmanship is the art of *making* things possible. That was Marian, a statesperson. On his deathbed, FDR's Cabinet Secretary Henry L. Stimson wrote, "The person who works for [her or] his goals, believing in their eventual attainment, while that person may suffer setback and even disaster, [she or] he will never know defeat. The only deadly sin I know is cynicism." Marian had faith in our cause as long as she lived. She never gave up.

Marian stated the verity plainly: "The Peace Tax Fund is a win-win proposal." The government gets its complete taxes from the conscientious objectors, and the latter get to obey their consciences. Moreover, the government does not have to spend enormous sums prosecuting, feeding and sheltering such citizens in prison. There is yet another gain for the government: the receipt of taxes which at present are legally avoided. If a conscientious objector has a profession which, if practiced, could earn high income, she or he could do bare subsistence work and be below the threshold of federal income tax. If such a person could practice her or his profession with a clear conscience, as a consequence the government would get more tax income.

This establishment, in law, of the principle of conscientious objection to military taxation was the sublime mission of our beloved Marian Franz; a holy cause that, in the words of Lincoln, she has "thus far so nobly advanced." We shall miss her bright eyes and sweet smile.

Betweeen 1964 and 1997, Andy Jacobs served fifteen terms in the U.S. Congress representing Indiana's Tenth District (Indianapolis). From 1991 until 1996 he was the lead sponsor of the U.S. Peace Tax Fund Bill.

Introduction

This book is about a moral quest. It is also about a woman who gave personality and vitality to that quest. The quest is to establish a legal way in the United States for the taxes of conscientious objectors not to be used for purposes of war. The woman is Marian Franz. The book is a tribute to her intelligence, skill, verve, and lifelong passion for peace and justice. The essays which follow are a collection of Marian's finest writing. First printed as newsletter columns, they are reprinted here to inspire and offer a glimpse of the wisdom, humor, and tenacity that marked Marian's twenty-three years as executive director of the National Campaign for a Peace Tax Fund.

Marian was a professional lobbyist whose flair for style and color always made a simple blue blazer look elegant and professional. And she was a mom who lounged in her pajamas with her feet up on the coffee table and loved to laugh. She was a Kansas girl whose horizons were broadened early on by the presence of German prisoners of war laboring on the family farm. She was a farm girl who came to understand the lives of the urban poor of Chicago's South Side. She strode the corridors of congressional power with panache. She believed deeply in the moral cause of the Peace Tax Fund she represented, and she understood its limitations within the broad spectrum of work for peace. She called it "my other child," but her own children never felt it to be in competition with the primacy of their places in her life.

As a representative of the Presbyterian Church (USA), I went on visits to congressional offices with her for fifteen years. I could barely keep the names straight of the staffers with whom we had appointments, but Marian knew the crises in their families and their moral and spiritual struggles. She never forgot to ask something which demonstrated to the staffers that she cared about them. With equal verve—and authority—she could say, "We're making appointments for next week, and I need you and you and you to come along," or "Give me a baby to hold—just one baby, all I need is one." She got down on the floor with her grandchildren, and she stood up for justice.

She had an extraordinary gift of knowing how to enter other people's worlds. She brought that to every area of her life: her children, her grandchildren, her friends, her overseas colleagues, her staff and young interns, the congressional staffs she visited, her church friends and their families, her husband Delton as his world caved in around him during his illness. Wherever she was, there she was fully present.

Marian and Delton came to Washington to establish the Washington Office of the Mennonite Central Committee. Delton got the credit for being its first director, but their commitment was very much a mutual one. Their work laid a foundation for years to come for the sacred witness of the historic peace churches in the nation's capital and around the world. A direct line leads from their work to the vital and ongoing witness for peace by the Mennonite Central Committee in these troubled times.

Those who work for peace face a broad array of tasks and challenges. They include slowing the environmental devastation which destabilizes communities, building skills in negotiation and conflict resolution, working against nuclear weapons proliferation, supporting the United Nations, developing educational opportunities and economic infrastructure which offer credible alternatives to violent radicalism, and reversing the radical growth of militarization of U.S. foreign policy.

Legalization of conscientious objection to war taxes is not an end in itself. It is morally important as an expression of religious freedom in this country. It provides consistency and supports the integrity of people who refuse to participate in the military for reasons of conscience. And it is an important public reminder that there are better things to do with public money than to pay for war.

Marian Franz deeply loved the community of historic peace churches into which she was born and understood the importance of its contribution to our society at large. She drew on its strength. She understood that she had to reach out beyond it if the peace tax legislation was ever going to pass. That is how we non-peace-church staff got involved. In my case, she worked with the General Assembly of the Presbyterian Church (USA) to pass a resolution mandating Washington church staff to work on the bill.

Conscientious objection to military taxation was a new and utterly foreign idea to most members of Congress, and their young staffers were usually frankly skeptical. Marian had to start from scratch with basic education on the subject. This frequently morphed into a dialogue on moral values, and quite often, the values shaping the staffer's own life. It took repeated visits, letters from constituents, follow-up literature, and all the other tools in Marian's considerable supply to change that initial skepticism into actual support of the bill.

"Money is fungible" was the most frequent objection we heard. Money can move around. The proposed bill does not actually reduce U.S. military spending; it merely diverts the money of conscientious objectors to nonviolent uses. Since the military budget would be met with other money, what difference would the bill make? This is a real limitation, a compromise that the campaign had to accept to make any headway at all. Congress is very protective of its responsibility to determine the federal budget. The idea that citizens have the power to make their own decisions about where tax money goes is simply unacceptable to many members of Congress. Building enough support to actually pass such a bill is like climbing a very high mountain. It will happen. It would have been wonderful for it to have happened in Marian's lifetime, but it did not. It is left to her successors and those who treasure her memory to move forward with her work.

Six of these successors, colleagues of Marian in her work for peace and justice, have contributed chapters to accompany Marian's essays in this book. These chapters add contemporary perspectives to the timeless quality of Marian's essays, underscore the importance of this cause and Marian's key role in it, and spell out some of the challenges that lie ahead in the struggle for a Peace Tax Fund.

After working more than two decades on behalf of conscience, Marian's final challenge came in the form of cancer. With all the determination of her personality, Marian fought her illness to the very end, to her last breath. That cancer may be out there somewhere gloating, thinking that it won the battle, but it did not. Her will to live, her refusal to complain despite the terrible pain, and her loving gratitude for her "angels" (the caretakers around her) won her the prize for dignity in the struggle, hands down. All the cancer could do, finally, was give her a kick down the road into the valley of the shadow of death, the road that took her home to God. For the rest of us, a light went out at her death in November 2006, but for her the dawn has come.

Barbara Green has served as executive director of the Churches' Center for Theology and Public Policy in Washington, D.C., since 1998. Previously, she was a policy advocate for the Presbyterian Church (USA), specializing in international relations and security policy. She is co-author of Lines in the Sand: Justice and the Gulf War.

Part I

CONTEMPORARY VOICES ON
CONSCIENCE, WAR, AND TAXES

Remembrance of Marian Franz and Her Leadership of the Effort to Enact Peace Tax Fund Legislation

DAVID R. BASSETT

How does one remember a person, now departed, with whom one has worked for a quarter century? I remember Marian Franz as leader, prophet, captain of the ship, and friend. We at the National Campaign for a Peace Tax Fund were so fortunate when Marian joined us.

In what follows, I shall report on some of the experiences in Marian's life which prepared her for the work which she began with the National Campaign for a Peace Tax Fund (NCPTF) in 1982. For twenty-three years, she led and expanded what began as a small movement, bringing it to national and international arenas. I shall also mention experiences from my life which resulted in development of the Peace Tax Fund legislation. And I shall describe how Marian joined these efforts and the ways in which she led the movement to pass the Peace Tax Fund Bill, legislation which aims to broaden the right of conscientious objection to include conscientious objection to military taxation (COMT).

Early period of Marian's life[1]

Marian was born on October 12, 1930, in Newton, Kansas, to Ernest and Justine Claassen, the third of their five children Edith, Vernon, Marian, Doris, and Joan. She grew up with her Mennonite family on a farm in rural Kansas, often walking several miles to and from school.

She has described (in her essay on page 80, titled " 'Enemies': Foes Today Can Be Friends Tomorrow") an especially formative experience. During World War II, there were German prisoners of war billeted in a small nearby town, assigned to help the local farmers with harvesting. She, a young teenager at the time, did not fear the "enemy" soldiers, but rather the U.S. guards, armed with guns and bayonets, who accompanied them. Marian writes of the friendly greeting (in German) her mother gave to the prisoners, as they came to work on her family's farm, and as her mother invited them in to her table at lunchtime. She describes

21

a number of ways in which the barriers between "guard" and "enemy" were eroded by the hospitality extended to them by her Mennonite home and community. Marian came to wonder if the German and U.S. soldiers were not each other's enemies; perhaps the real enemy was the system of war.

Marian went to Bethel College in North Newton, Kansas, receiving a bachelor's degree in social sciences and religion in 1954. Also that year, she married Delton Franz. In the years to come, they had three children—a son, Gregory, and two daughters, Gayle and Coretta.

Delton and Marian both served brief pastorates in Kansas. They then moved to Chicago, where Marian attended Mennonite Biblical Seminary, obtaining a master's degree in religious education in 1957. In Chicago, Delton and Marian helped to found an interracial Mennonite church and were active in the civil rights movement. In the late 1950s and into the 1960s, Marian worked for the Church Federation of Greater Chicago and became director of Weekday Religious Education. She worked in cooperation with the public schools, having responsibility for one-third of the area of Chicago.

In 1968, Delton and Marian moved to Washington, D.C., where Delton became the Washington Representative of the Mennonite Central Committee's Peace Section office, located across the street from the Capitol in the Methodist Building. Marian began lobbying work on human rights issues, including lobbying with the Friends Committee on National Legislation. In 1971, she helped to found Dunamis, and became its first director. Dunamis, a Christian organization that spoke to policymakers about political issues facing the nation, was one of many organizations arising from the vision of Rev. Gordon Cosby, founder of the Church of the Saviour in Washington, D.C. During her years in Dunamis, Marian worked on developing pastoral/prophetic relationships with members of Congress concerned with social issues. Marian was active in Dunamis during the height of the Vietnam War, a war which affected communities around the world.

Beginnings of the Peace Tax Fund legislative approach

It was during the Vietnam War era that the first steps were taken toward initiating peace tax fund legislation.[2] In 1966, two Quaker families from Ann Arbor, Michigan, Friends Meeting—Johan and Frances Eliot, and Robert and Margaret Blood—realized that they could not, in conscience, allow their income tax dollars to be used for funding the Vietnam

War. They joined others around the country in the war tax resistance movement. In addition to their war tax resistance action, the Bloods and the Eliots gave thought to a legislative initiative. They sought the help of a Quaker law student at the University of Michigan Law School, Thomas Towe, persuading him to prepare a brief to be used as part of a bill which might be submitted to Congress, recognizing the right of conscientious objection to military taxation.

Our family moved to Ann Arbor in 1968 and joined the Friends Meeting there. In June 1970, at the annual meeting of the Lake Erie Yearly Meeting (LEYM) (of which the Ann Arbor Meeting was a member) a minute was approved, to be shared with all monthly meetings in LEYM, which asked Friends to consider, in the light of the Quaker peace testimony, the implications of paying for war through their federal taxes. This minute was brought to Ann Arbor Meeting in summer 1970 by its clerk, Mabel Hamm. I was among those who heard the minute. Being a conscientious objector to participation in war (having performed two years of alternative service in 1955–1957, as a physician serving with the American Friends Service Committee Community Development project in Barpali, Orissa, India), I was struck with the importance of this minute.

I pondered whether we should engage in war tax resistance, bring the issue of COMT into the courts, or try to change U.S. tax law as it related to federal taxes used for military purposes. My wife (Miyoko Inouye Bassett) and I decided that we would begin to withhold the portion of our federal taxes used for current military expenditures (even though we knew that the government would ultimately seize these funds, plus penalty and interest), and that we should explore the possibility of legislative change. We realized that there was no way to gauge the amount of time and effort this would take, nor the ways it would compete with the medical work which my wife and I were doing at the University of Michigan.

This pondering led to discussions I had with Roger Lind, a professor of social work at the University of Michigan, who had experience with lobbying Congress. Lind knew of the work of Professor Joseph Sax, at the University of Michigan Law School and that he had gone to Sweden to speak with American draft resisters who had moved to Sweden rather than to fight in a war which they opposed. On the basis of this information, I contacted Professor Sax to ask if he might help us to draft legislation which would extend the concept of conscientious objection to military service to COMT. He found one of his law students who could work with us, and, in January 1971, Michael Hall, Professor Sax, and I began the discussions which led to the early drafts of what became the World Peace Tax Fund Bill.

Much of the preliminary brief came from the work done by Thomas Towe. It was Professor Sax's recommendation that the basic construct of the legislation be based on a trust fund mechanism. The bill was constructed such that any U.S. citizen taxpayer who was conscientiously opposed to participation in all war could be recognized by the government, following the same criteria used by the Selective Service System for those applying as conscientious objectors to military service. Such citizens would still pay the full amount of their income, estate, or gift taxes, but these taxes would be appropriated by Congress only for non-military purposes.

We obtained support for the World Peace Tax Fund Bill from the Ann Arbor Friends Meeting in the summer of 1971, and from Ann Arbor's Interfaith Council for Peace in September 1971. With this encouragement, we formed a working committee which met frequently in our home, and we began to make trips to Washington, D.C., to seek potential congressional sponsors of the World Peace Tax Fund Bill.

It is likely that in 1971 Marian began to hear of these efforts. In October 1971, I came to Washington, D.C., with the hope of speaking with leaders of several organizations (Brethren, Mennonite, Methodist, and Quaker) whom I felt might be willing and able to support the introduction, in Congress, of the World Peace Tax Fund Bill. One of the first visits I made was to the Washington Office of the Mennonite Central Committee, where I was warmly welcomed by Delton Franz, director of the office. After I presented the concept and the genesis of the bill, Delton conveyed that he was prepared to work with us, and that he would seek the necessary support from Mennonite Central Committee and its constituents.

Additional visits with the Church of the Brethren office, the Friends Committee on National Legislation (FCNL), and the Methodist legislative offices indicated sufficient support so that I felt we could take the next step, which was to plan a meeting of many interested persons and groups in the Washington area. That meeting was hosted by FCNL in January, 1972, by which time we had received assurance from Representative Ronald Dellums that he was prepared to introduce the World Peace Tax Fund Bill into Congress and to find additional co-sponsors. Much of the groundwork with Representative Dellums, his staff, and other representatives who also became original co-sponsors—such as Charles Rangel and John Conyers Jr.—was done by Roger Lind, who had become a member of the Ann Arbor working group. Lind knew the importance of working with members of the newly formed Black Caucus, many of whom supported the nonviolent approaches of Martin Luther King, Jr.

At the January 1972, meeting at FCNL, we agreed upon the plan of carrying on the organizational work in Ann Arbor for a few years, but with the intent, after some funds were raised, of finding a location for an office in Washington, D.C., for the organization which we would call the National Council for a World Peace Tax Fund (NCPTF). In addition to finding a suitable site, the plans were to find staff, create a board of directors, appoint officers, and hold periodic meetings in Washington.

The World Peace Tax Fund Bill was introduced on April 17, 1972, as H.R. 14414, with Ronald Dellums as lead sponsor and nine other co-sponsors. The Ann Arbor Working Group continued to be active, creating a newsletter, beginning to make regional and national contacts, seeking funding, and attending and speaking at regional and national meetings. A Washington-based steering committee was also formed, with one of the active members being Leah Felton, who also worked part-time at the FCNL office.

In April 1975, it was possible to move most of the files from Ann Arbor to the new Washington office of the NCPTF, located in space made available to us at modest rental from the Friends Meeting of Washington.[3] The location at 2121 Decatur Place, NW, on the grounds of the Friends Meeting (three office rooms, with the possibility of holding larger meetings in other areas of the Friends Meeting property—and with the entire area being conveniently near the Dupont Circle Metro Station) promised to be an effective location and has remained so to this date.

Beginning in 1975, and over the next seven years, we found three dedicated persons to staff the Washington office. Bill Samuel, Sister Mary Rae Waller, and William Strong (in that sequence, and with volunteer staff) coordinated the many activities needed to begin our legislative, outreach and educational activities. We also held board meetings semiannually, with representatives mostly from those Washington-based organizations which were supportive of the Peace Tax Fund effort. One of the persons serving as chair, from 1977 to 1979, was Delton Franz, whose leadership and knowledge of legislative processes was invaluable.

Our search for an executive director to follow Bill Strong's planned one-year period at the NCPTF office (1981-82) was rewarded by a fortunate development, whose significance we hardly realized at the time.

Marian's tenure as executive director of NCPTF

In September 1982, Marian Franz became the first full-time executive director of NCPTF. At that time, she was joined in the office by Jean Cooper, administrative assistant, and Leah Felton. The new chair of the NCPTF board was Robert Hull, of Newton, Kansas, secretary of peace and justice of the General Conference Mennonite Church.

While Marian faced all the challenges common to any director of a small non-governmental organization, it is remarkable to contemplate the skill and energy with which she approached her work. In addition to her administrative and educational duties, she was the lobbyist for the Peace Tax Fund Bill. She sought, trained, and supported the other office staff members; extended the organization's outreach to many Congressional districts; expanded fundraising; established close contacts with a number of interested organizations; created friendly ties with members of the NCPTF board throughout the year and at semiannual board meetings; and established a long-term working relationship with members of the Friends Meeting of Washington.

Appendix B sets forth many of the important developments with which Marian was involved. One aspect of Marian's work not included in this listing are the many talks which Marian gave around the country in support of the Peace Tax Fund Bill and its underlying concepts. From the beginning of her tenure, Marian traveled often, and to many states, addressing denominational and non-religious conferences and gatherings. She maintained a focus on both building support for the legislative initiative and also challenging citizens to examine world problems with a nonviolent, rather than militaristic, mindset.

Soon after Marian began her work, the NCPTF newsletter began reporting developments relating to COMT in New Zealand, the United Kingdom, West Germany, and, later, in multiple countries. It is worth noting that NCPTF staff member Leah Felton had lived in the Netherlands for several years beginning in July 1975. During this time she was in contact with Dutch peace workers who were protesting NATO's decision to place 572 missiles in Western Europe. Leah informed persons in the Dutch Movement for the Refusal of Military Taxes of the legislative efforts in the U.S., building a cooperative relationship between the two nations. (In 1988, the second International Conference on War Tax Resistance and Peace Tax Campaigns was held in Vierhouten, the Netherlands.)

NCPTF ties to the international COMT movement began more formally in 1986, when Marian and I attended the first International Conference on War Tax Resistance and Peace Tax Campaigns, held in Tübingen, West Germany. Each of these international conferences, held every two years since 1986, has provided opportunities for collaborating with persons from other nations, working both on legislative efforts and in the area of war tax resistance (WTR). As Ruth Benn mentions in her chapter on WTR, there are some war tax resisters who see little role for peace tax fund legislation. But Marian, through conversations at the international conferences, in other international bodies over the decades, and with the National War Tax Resistance Coordinating Committee in the U.S., contributed significantly to maintaining friendly relationships between the WTR and the legislative components of the COMT movement.

An important aspect of Marian's work, throughout her time with NCPTF, had to do with her intellectual capacities, combined with deep spiritual roots and practical down-to-earth skills, and the ways she called upon these attributes to inform all aspects of her work. The essays in this book are a clear example of her capacity to see a multitude of issues up close and at the same time from a very broad perspective. Her ability to express her understandings in words are evident in her essays and were also evident in her spoken messages, which were informative and often very moving.

Another aspect of her work in directing the activities of NCPTF (and of the Peace Tax Foundation, once it was created in 1985) had to do with her choosing, training, and supporting staff (both paid and volunteer) in these two organizations. In addition to setting wise standards for work performance, she maintained a friendly atmosphere in the small NCPTF office. Especially in the later years of her tenure, with her own children now adult and her husband, Delton, at home with a progressive illness, Marian regarded her coworkers very much as "family," resulting in a special sense of camaraderie and mutual support. For board members, the aspects both of this sense of a "working family," as well as the inspiration which came from knowing the breadth and scope of Marian's work, were a very palpable experience. We felt this at each of our board meetings; as we received the latest newsletters; and as we carried on our interactions with our own constituents, and Marian, in the times between board meetings.

An important part of Marian's work on behalf of the COMT movement, in the international arena, was her testimony delivered to the UN Commission on Human Rights. This became possible after June 1999, when Conscience and Peace Tax International (CPTI), the international body dedicated to war tax resistance issues and to peace tax campaigns, was granted "special consultative status" as an NGO in the UN's Economic and Social Council. Marian attended several meetings of this body at the UN in New York and in Europe. Marian also played an important leadership role in CPTI. She was vice chair from the beginning of CPTI in 1994, became acting chair in 2004, and was to serve as chair at the eleventh International Conference, held October 26-29, 2006 in Woltersdorf, near Berlin, Germany. However, illness prevented her from attending this conference.

In 2005, several events came together which led Marian to decide that she should step down from her role as executive director at the end of the year (though she hoped that she could continue with her lobbying efforts on a part-time basis.) These events included the surgery which she had undergone for cancer and Delton's progressive illness. (He died in March 2006.)

The NCPTF board of directors then made plans to appoint Tim Godshall as interim executive director, for the period January 1 through June 30, 2006. (Tim had worked with Marian since March 2003.) A search for the next executive director led to our selecting Alan Gamble to follow Tim Godshall as executive director, beginning on June 1, 2006. Alan was able to have some overlap with Tim and to have a few meetings with Marian. But, by the summer of 2006, Marian was suffering from recurrent cancer and was unable to provide for as much transition in responsibilities as she had hoped.

Marian died on November 17, 2006, after a two-year struggle with cancer. Her loss was widely noted and greatly felt. A memorial service for Marian was held at Hyattsville (Md.) Mennonite Church on February 17, 2007.

In the addresses she gave over the years, there are a number of messages Marian stated many times. I record here three of her statements, which she leaves as a legacy:

No witness for conscience is ever lost.

War taxes kill twice. First, they directly enable war—particularly by paying for weapons. Second, taxes allocated for war represent a distortion of priorities. Money is taken away from the important work of healing, and is spent to destroy and kill.

The Religious Freedom Peace Tax Fund Bill is a way to protect the religious freedom and the rights of conscience of that minority of taxpayers whose religious and moral principles forbid their participation in war in any form.

I close with words of tribute, spoken by Representative John Lewis, who became the lead sponsor of the Religious Freedom Peace Tax Fund Bill in 1998:

Marian was a tireless voice for religious freedom and the rights of people of conscience. Her energy and persistence in advocating for the Religious Freedom Peace Tax Fund was a reflection of her deep commitment to democracy and to the cause of peace.

David R. Bassett has been a conscientious objector to war since the early 1950s, when he performed alternative civilian service as a physician in India with the American Friends Service Committee. From 1957 to 2002, his medical work was directed to the prevention of cardiovascular disease at the Universities of Pennsylvania, Hawaii, and Michigan. Since 1975 he has served on the Board of the National Campaign for a Peace Tax Fund.

---

1. Material in this section is drawn from remembrances of Marian in the *Mennonite Weekly Review,* Nov. 27, 2006; National Campaign for a Peace Tax Fund website (*www.peacetaxfund.org*), posted Nov. 30, 2006; National War Tax Resistance Coordinating Committee's *More Than a Paycheck,* Feb., 2007; and *www.washingtonpost.com* obituary notice published Dec. 13, 2006.

2. These steps are described in chapter 6 in the *Handbook on Military Taxes and Conscience,* published in 1988 by the Friends Committee on War Tax Concerns.

3. In 1994, most of the Peace Tax Fund files remaining in Ann Arbor were

relocated to the Bentley Historical Library at the University of Michigan. The Bentley Library is a repository for documents from many sources, describing organizations and movements which had their origins, or important aspects of their origin, in Michigan. These are available for review by interested persons, in that library. The Peace Tax Fund documents are listed under the heading David R. Bassett, Donor No. 8242; Papers, 1963-1994.

Conscientious Objection to Military Taxation as Derived from Conscientious Objection to Military Service

L. WILLIAM YOLTON

From her childhood, the true tales of suffering for conscience born of religious conviction were part of Marian Franz's history. She was told of young men in World War I who suffered for their beliefs and, in a few cases, died and were returned to their communities from prison at Alcatraz. When their coffins were opened, the young Hutterites were clad in the very uniforms for which they had died rather than wear. She lived through the prejudices of World War II—yellow paint slathered on meeting houses and hostility toward believers in traditions that objected to participation in military service. As one of the first Mennonite women to have theological training, Marian's understanding was undergirded by faith and informed by reason. That preparation suited her well for her leadership in the campaign for a Peace Tax Fund.

The origins in America of conscientious objection to military service were faith-based, not derived from secular human rights or natural law. The objections were to participation in the "worldly" evils, instead of life in the holy commonwealth or the commitment to a gathered community of the redeemed. As Martin Luther "turned the monastery into the world," the Anabaptists and—a century later—the Quakers and Shakers became the monastery "in the world, but not of the world." There they practiced the "evangelical counsels," on renewed, biblical grounds. Their community was a sanctuary in which they sought to be a peaceable kingdom.

Participation in the coercion and violence of the state and its system of military force was shunned by participants in the radical reformation. The peace churches developed a "two kingdoms" doctrine, consisting of a worldly realm and a divinely appointed kingdom. Thus it was not so much that war was forbidden (since it was inevitable in the worldly kingdom), but the believers' *participation in* the military, which involved a submission to the instrument of worldly authority, and was therefore a rejection of the gospel of peace.

Thus, the current law, the Military Selective Service Act of 1967, which provides for conscientious objection to military service, is properly focused on objection to participation in military service. It is that religious practice and belief which is protected by the First Amendment.

The narrow exemption of traditional pacifist religious believers from combatant service because they belonged to *communities of belief*, which was the standard during World War I, was expanded in World War II to allow those believers (based on those same personal beliefs) to be allowed to do alternative service as civilians. And then, during the Vietnam War this was further expanded to more broadly understand qualifying religious belief and allow for *individualized* alternative service. The understanding that afforded conscientious objector status due to *group* membership has shifted, due to First Amendment analysis that no religion can be "established," and now allows for eligibility based on *individual* beliefs.

The beginning of the Peace Tax Fund movement in the early 1970s, which was influenced significantly by the desire to stop funding the Vietnam War, has moved to its philosophical and constitutional core by making an analogy with current law that supports conscientious objection to military service on the grounds of religious belief. The underlying rationale for the Religious Freedom Peace Tax Fund (RFPTF) Bill, and its earlier versions, is that just as the law protects the consciences of those who are conscripted bodily to military service, so the law should protect those whose consciences object to conscripting their labor for war, in the form of taxes. To many conscientious objectors, the conscription of the fruits of their labor for military purposes, though further removed, is just as objectionable in principle as bodily conscription.

Just as conscription law now allows for alternative service by conscripts, so alternative service for "conscripted" tax dollars should be accommodated. Proponents of the RFPTF Bill are not trying to get out of paying taxes, just the conflicting purpose for which those taxes are levied. The proposed legislation does not attempt to tell Congress where those tax dollars are to be diverted. Analogous to alternative service, the legislation instructs Congress to allocate funds in ways that are consistent with the reasons for objection to military taxation, which are rooted in religious objection to military service.

As far back as the seventeenth century, colonial statutes exempted pacifist sects from military service. Massachusetts was first in 1657, followed by Rhode Island in 1662. During the Revolutionary War, when all able-bodied men were required to join the Continental Army, George

Washington dismissed from the militia conscripts who were from traditional peace churches.

In World War I the U.S. allowed conscientious objection (as a non-combatant in the Army) only to those with membership in traditional pacifist religious bodies. At this point, religious objectors qualified as participants in a *communally* held belief. (Even in the Vietnam War era, believers from the traditional peace churches were approved by some draft boards merely on the basis of their membership in peace churches, without the required individual testimony to their beliefs.) Others who did not have such a membership, or whom the Army did not approve for non-combatant military service, or who objected to such non-combatant service went to prison. Individuals, notably Evan Thomas, the brother of Norman Thomas, could not be accepted as conscientious objectors, and instead suffered torturing conditions in prison.

During World War II, the Burke-Wadsworth Act recognized an *individual* right to conscientious objector status and provided for alternative service either as a civilian or as a non-combatant in the military. As a result, not only members of the peace churches qualified but several thousands from other religious bodies. In a compromise with the government, the peace churches bore the cost of the maintenance of the Civilian Public Service camps where conscientious objectors did their alternative service. During the course of the war, conscientious objectors were allowed to be attendants at mental hospitals and began the movement to reform the U.S. mental health system.

Finally, in *U.S. v. Seeger* (1965) the Supreme Court expanded eligibility to those who did not have conventional religious beliefs. In a lengthy opinion buttressed by theologians, the court allowed conscientious objector status for those with "moral and ethical beliefs that occupied the same place in their lives as did the beliefs of those who clearly qualified." Thus the court did not so much change the standard for qualifying as expand the definition of religion. While the beliefs may include philosophical, sociological and political elements, they must be essentially religious. The statute on conscientious objection was revised in 1967 to incorporate the court's decision. As a result of this history, the standard for qualifying as a conscientious objector to military taxation includes those whose "deeply held" moral, ethical, or religious beliefs will not allow them to participate in war.

Around this same time, the Vietnam War was heating up. Equipped with the new statute on conscientious objection, draft counselors on college campuses across the country looked for ways to keep students out of the unpopular war. In addition to many student deferments, some young men went to seminary to stay out of the draft. Other reflective individuals looked to conscientious objection as a way to meet their obligations for service while honoring their convictions. The churches worked to develop community-based counseling to shift the support for counseling to all who might qualify and need advice about their options. A great many creative alternative service positions were innovated.

An individual seeking conscientious objector status had to demonstrate that he could not serve in the military "on the basis of religious training and belief ... [such that] it would give him no rest or peace to be any part of an instrument of war." This "training and belief" requirement prevented individuals from claiming conscientious objector status for reasons of "expediency," which the statute prohibited. Demonstrating such a basis for qualifying was often difficult for those young men just beyond puberty who had no participation in pacifist religious communities. (Similarly, those desiring to qualify as "designated conscientious objectors" so as to have their "tax payments used for nonmilitary purposes," under the provisions of the RFPTF Bill, will have to show the background for their beliefs to qualify for the tax diversion.)

The history of the development of the Peace Tax Fund legislation, which has resulted in the RFPTF Bill, still assumes that the instrument of war is related to military service, made possible either by one's bodily involvement, or, as Marian Franz tagged it, by one's "conscripted dollars." Thus the evolved title of the present RFPTF Bill is founded on objection to military taxation. It stays close to the evolution of the legislated right to conscientious objection to "participation in war in any form" as defined by the Military Selective Service Act (50 U.S.C. App 456 (j)).

The current bill is focused on religious objection to military taxation and the thousands who would take advantage of such a bill to divert their taxes to alternative service for life rather than for the instruments of war. Not only would absolute pacifists qualify but also those who believe that there might be no modern wars that meet the qualifications of just war teaching. Such persons can make an argument that they are opposed to "participation in war in any form." Many such conscientious objectors have emerged from religious traditions such as Protestant, Catholic, and Islamic, which have traditions of just war and even holy war. This is a result of the increased support for explicit belief and new rational understandings of the connections of faith to life as held by the individual believer.

Provisions for conscientious objection are *constitutionally* founded on the First Amendment clause guaranteeing the "free exercise of religion." The Supreme Court has viewed the law about conscientious objection as a *legislated* privilege, and has not yet fully addressed its support in the Constitution. We do take note that the Court based the expansion of the law in *U.S. v. Seeger* on the First Amendment. Scholars and advocates do see conscientious objection (to military service, and to military taxation) as founded in the First Amendment free exercise clause in the Constitution. Will it come to be recognized as a human right? This question, addressed by Derek Brett later in this book, is still evolving toward another chapter in the moral development of the human race.

Rev. L. William Yolton is executive director emeritus of the Center on Conscience and War (formerly known as the National Service Board for Religious Objectors, and then as the National Interreligious Service Board for Conscientious Objectors).

References

L. William Yolton, "Conscientious Objection," in *Protest, Power and Change: An Encyclopedia of Nonviolent Action*, ed. Roger S. Powers et. al (New York and London: Garland, 1997), pp. 125-128.

L. William Yolton, "Pacifism," in *International Military and Defense Encyclopedia*, ed. Trevor N. Dupuy (Washington and London: Brassey's, 1993).

War Tax Resistance and
the Peace Tax Fund

RUTH BENN

Marian Franz began her tenure at the National Campaign for a Peace Tax Fund (NCPTF) in 1982. In September that year she attended the conference on war tax resistance that founded the National War Tax Resistance Coordinating Committee (NWTRCC). NCPTF was one of NWTRCC's early affiliate organizations, and NWTRCC's statement of purpose includes a pledge to support those who work for a Peace Tax Fund Bill.

Refusal to pay for war long predates the founding of NWTRCC. There is little reason to doubt that whenever the first tax was levied to pay for war, more than one person refused to pay for reasons of conscience. This is well illustrated in the Aristophanes play *Lysistrata* from 411 BCE, in which Greek women argue against paying money for war. It follows that the idea for peace tax fund legislation grew out of the lack of a legal alternative for people who owed taxes but could not, in conscience, pay for war.

For centuries a specific tax was levied for a specific war. Eventually governments realized that hiding the costs of war made waging war all the more palatable, and today we have a system where taxes are pooled into a general fund and disbursed to the various branches of the government. In many ways this has complicated war tax resistance, and it makes sense that a legislative option evolved that would allow taxpayers to support only the non-military portions of the budget, the Peace Tax Fund Bill.

Refusing to pay federal taxes is an act of civil disobedience, whether one refuses a small, symbolic amount; the military percentage of taxes due; or the full tax bill. Thousands, perhaps millions, of people grapple with their consciences over having to pay taxes when they are deeply opposed to either a particular war (such as the invasion of Iraq) or all war. Although only a small number choose war tax refusal, those who do have come to feel it is the only way to withdraw their participation from war and to register the strongest protest possible. In his "Letter from a Birmingham Jail," Martin Luther King, Jr., wrote of the benefit of such protest: "Nonviolent direct action seeks to create such a crisis and foster such a creative tension that a community which has constantly refused to negotiate is forced to confront the issue. It seeks so to dramatize the issue that it can no longer be ignored."

Members of the war tax resistance network hold a variety of views on the legislative approach to address military taxation. Some oppose spending time on lobbying and legislation; some are ambivalent; and some war tax resisters actively support the Peace Tax Fund Bill and help with its promotion and lobbying.

Reasons expressed by those who oppose legislative work include the following:

- It's an "easy out" for people who are not comfortable that their taxes go to war but are fearful of refusing to pay. Working for the bill assuages their guilt.

- Many resisters are not religious, so when the Peace Tax Fund Bill was rewritten to align more closely with the First Amendment right to freedom of religious expression, they felt more alienated from it. (This re-write followed the passage of the Religious Freedom Restoration Act in 1993. For more information, see essay on page 132.)

- Any process that gives government bodies the power to decide who is a conscientious objector (CO) will create a process that forces people to resist anyway. The problems military personnel have today in finding out about CO options and applying for a CO discharge bear out this fear.

- The adage "war is the health of the state" is taken seriously among war tax resisters who tend toward an anarchist philosophy. There is little point in seeking permission from an inherently corrupt system.

However, there are also many war tax resisters who hope the Religious Freedom Peace Tax Fund Bill will pass and work for it for the same reasons expressed by all of its supporters. They just cannot wait for the government to tell them when it's okay not to pay for war. Refusal to pay some or all of their taxes combined with lobbying for the Religious Freedom Peace Tax Fund Bill is the right combination for them.

The examples of all kinds of dedicated war tax resisters become the argument for why such a bill is needed, in the view of Peace Tax Fund lobbyists. There are people who live below a taxable income so as to not pay for war. There are people who live outside the system, earning money off the books and adjusting their lives so as not to get pulled into a process that supports war. There are people who file and openly refuse to pay, risking IRS seizures of money and property. Many have had houses and cars taken and bank accounts wiped out, but they continue to refuse to pay for war voluntarily. These people are the arguments for the Religious Freedom Peace Tax Fund Bill.

Marian Franz understood the range of viewpoints among war tax resisters. She was prepared to respond when a new generation of resisters came along and challenged the details of the bill or the time spent on lobbying government officials. Marian respected whatever nonviolent approach an individual wanted to take to respond to the problem of war and taxes, but she knew where she wanted to focus. At the 2005 war tax resistance strategy conference, Marian noted how much she enjoyed lobbying: "You all can go to whatever mission fields you want; give me the United States Congress!" She believed in the bill, its potential to influence change, and the relief it would bring to thousands who struggle with their consciences over paying military taxes to the federal government.

NWTRCC is a resource and support center that pulls together under its umbrella a disparate network of people who refuse to pay for war and the groups around the country that work on or support this issue. It has no government-sponsored nonprofit status and remains aloof from the associated regulations. NCPTF is more tightly focused on legislation and lobbying. Despite these differences, the two groups have had a long and friendly relationship—sharing presentations at conferences and workshops, working together to plan the 2000 International Conference on War Tax Resistance and Peace Tax Campaigns in Washington, D.C., carrying articles and announcements in each other's newsletters, attending each other's special events, linking between websites, and sharing ideas for new projects or programs.

NWTRCC and NCPTF have worked in harmony since 1982, each equally anxious to stop forced taxation for military purposes and bring about dramatic change in the government's ability to finance war. In the quest for a peaceful world, the paths we choose at times run parallel, cross, or join together for miles on end. Sometimes along the way things get bumpy, and while some give up, others keep pushing along. Marian Franz stayed on her path with a dedication that serves as an example for us all.

Ruth Benn has been resisting war taxes since the 1980s. She is a former staff member of the War Resisters League and the current coordinator for the National War Tax Resistance Coordinating Committee, which is based in Brooklyn, New York.

A Legislative Perspective on the Peace Tax Fund Bill

EDWARD F. SNYDER

Why, after some thirty-six years of vigorous and well-directed effort, has it not been possible to achieve the right of conscientious objectors to avoid paying taxes for war? Bluntly speaking, I would say it is because the group seeking this right is relatively small and politically insignificant in the Washington world of big money and bureaucratic inertia, and because this group must deal with the general congressional antipathy to pacifism.

By all rights the effort should have been successful by now. It is a classic case of the First Amendment right of citizens to petition the government for a redress of grievances. It sprang from the deep convictions of certain individuals who obtained expert legal assistance to draft a bill. The language was taken to Washington, where representatives of sympathetic organizations, members of Congress, and their staff fine-tuned the proposal. Congressional co-sponsors were sought and obtained. It was introduced in the House of Representatives in 1972 near the time of the income tax deadline and referred to the Ways and Means Committee. In the following years the bill was introduced in each Congress with additional co-sponsors. Modifications were made to make it acceptable to more members of Congress. Testimony was presented to relevant congressional committees. Every year supporters came to Washington to educate themselves and lobby on Capitol Hill. Peace Tax Fund staff and committee members traveled the country speaking. Additional supporting organizations, religious and secular, were obtained.

And yet, and yet—House cosponsors in any one year never exceeded fifty-five, and only six Senators have signed on over the years. Why?

I believe there is a general reluctance in Congress and the executive branch to disturb the fragile public compliance with the federal tax system. An IRS witness in 1992 told a Ways and Means subcommittee that the Peace Tax Fund would create "problems of complexity, confusion, and increased administrative burden." That witness maintained that taxpayers might inappropriately claim conscientious objector (CO) status and, if they were allowed to designate the uses for which their tax dollars are spent, "our entire budgetary process would be undermined" with probable loss of revenue for needed programs.

In addition, the federal judiciary has consistently given primacy to the financial needs of the nation state over the First Amendment protection of the religious freedom even of a small minority, the recognition of whose rights could not possibly threaten national security. My personal experience in challenging and losing a case applying the "frivolous tax penalty" of $500 or more for a claim based on deep moral convictions made me very aware of judicial readiness to support the IRS' rejection of the CO position.[1] This reinforces the need to petition Congress to recognize conscientious objectors' refusal to pay for war.

In Congress, many liberals who might be expected to support the rights of conscientious objectors have given primary allegiance to maintaining federal revenues to assure needed health, housing, food, environmental, and other social programs. Many conservatives have seen the Peace Tax Fund legislation as a threat to the huge military spending programs. Both have used the "floodgates" argument: If an exception is made so CO taxpayers can choose how some of their income tax dollars are spent, soon all sorts of interest groups will want exceptions. The floodgates will open and soon the lake of taxpayer money will be drained or diverted from congressional intent. (The checkoff for the Presidential Election Campaign Fund on IRS Form 1040 gives taxpayers the right to direct a small portion of their tax dollars, but this is not seen as relevant.)

To me, the floodgates argument is one of the easiest to answer logically. There would be no loss of federal revenues. CO claimants would pay the full amount of taxes owed, but the military percentage would go to governmental purposes that don't violate their religious beliefs about the taking of human life. Objections based on political, economic, or social considerations don't pass this test. The only possible exceptions would be for those people who do not want their federal tax dollars to go for abortions or for capital punishment. But even if the cost of such federal programs, if any, could be identified, their cost to individual taxpayers would be in pennies rather than the hundreds or thousands of tax dollars individuals pay for war purposes. Indeed, the Congressional Research Service said in 1974 that the Peace Tax Fund proposal "would not open a Pandora's box to claims by other persons." And the Congressional Joint

Committee on Taxation in 1992 and 1994 certified that a proposal like the Peace Tax Fund Bill would increase federal revenues due to voluntary compliance by taxpayers.

Conversely, some ardent peace activists oppose the Peace Tax Fund because it does *not* reduce military spending. They believe that nonpayment of war taxes is the only moral course. I personally see no necessary conflict between war tax resistance and working for peace tax fund legislation. Indeed, the greater the number of resisters, the greater the likelihood the government will seriously consider legislation making an exemption for conscientious objectors. The number of tax resisters during the war in Indochina was a closely guarded IRS secret that even congressional offices couldn't discover.

The story of how the CO provision was inserted in the draft law is instructive. In World War I, religious and nonreligious objectors suffered severe community and military pressures, discrimination, and violence. There was no provision for conscientious objectors and no provision for non-military service. Many who were drafted refused to serve. In the end, many hundreds of conscientious objectors were mistreated and imprisoned, and some even died in prison. So much sand was thrown in the gears, so much military effort was diverted to dealing with this minority, that when the draft law for World War II was written, the recognition for conscientious objection was inserted in the law. That provision, now 50 U.S.C. App 456 (j), the Military Selective Service Act, is the language on which the Peace Tax Fund Bill is based.

Congressional bills and sponsors

The Peace Tax Fund Bill has been introduced in every Congress since the Ninety-Second in 1972.[2] Representative Ronald Dellums of California was the lead sponsor of the first Peace Tax Fund Bill (introduced as H.R. 14414 on April 17, 1972). Dellums, Representative Ben Rosenthal of New York, and I spoke at a press conference on that date (the income tax deadline that year.) There were eight additional congressional sponsors: Charles Rangel, Bella Abzug, Jonathan Bingham, and Bill Ryan of New York; Bob Kastenmeier of Wisconsin; John Conyers and Charles Diggs of Michigan; and Parren Mitchell of Maryland. Half of the original sponsors were members of the Congressional Black Caucus. This group, which is especially sensitive to minority rights, has formed the core group of Peace Tax Fund sponsors over the years. In addition, members of Congress with strong commitments to civil liberties and/or peace were often sponsors.

Later, after the National Campaign for a Peace Tax Fund (NCPTF) staff organized people around the country to put pressure on their representatives in Congress, sponsors included members who might not agree with the policy, but who understood the importance of this issue to some of their constituents.

In 1973 Dellums was joined by eleven other co-sponsors. In 1975 there were twenty-seven cosponsors. The number of House sponsors continued to grow with fluctuations between thirty and fifty-five. Lead sponsors in the House after Dellums included James Oberstar, Minn.; Don Bonker, Wash.; Doug Waldren, Pa.; Andy Jacobs, Ind.; and since 1998, John Lewis, Ga.

In 1977 Mark Hatfield of Oregon introduced the Peace Tax Fund Bill in the Senate as S. 880. This began his unwavering support for the Peace Tax Fund based on his deep personal religious views. His leadership was crucial in giving the proposal strong bipartisan support. From 1977 to 1996, under his steadfast leadership there were an equal number of Senate sponsors on both sides of the aisle: Republicans Hatfield; Charles Mathias, Md.; and Lowell Weicker Jr., Conn.; and Democrats Tom Harkin, Iowa; Mike Gravel, Ark.; and Paul Wellstone, Minn.

Over the years some changes have been made in the legislation to meet various objections and to gain more supporters. In 1985 the name was changed from the "World Peace Tax Fund Bill" to the "U.S. Peace Tax Fund Bill." The NCPTF Board of Directors noted that organizations in other nations had been uncomfortable with the use of the word "World" in the bill's name.

In 1993, with leadership from Andy Jacobs, the legislation was modified to remove the provision for a Peace Tax Fund Board, which had been given authority to receive proposals and disburse funds to relevant projects. Members of Congress were uneasy with a body outside Congress allocating federal funds. A short list of four popular programs was named instead—two domestic: Head Start and WIC (the special nutritional program for Women, Infants and Children), and two international: the Peace Corps and the U.S. Institute of Peace.

In 1998, under John Lewis' leadership, the bill was simplified in an attempt to meet IRS objections, and renamed the "Religious Freedom Peace Tax Fund Bill" to emphasize the bill's basis in the First Amendment right to free exercise of religion. The designation of the four specific programs as recipients was removed and the wording "allocated to any appropriation not for a military purpose" was substituted.

Hearings

After introduction in the House and Senate, bills are referred to the appropriate committees, then possibly to subcommittees, where many die at the end of the session. Peace Tax Fund bills were customarily referred to the Ways and Means Committee in the House, and the Finance Committee in the Senate. (At one time the House bill was also referred to the Education and Labor Committee and the Foreign Affairs Committee.) The next step is to hold hearings. Much of the work of Marian Franz and other staff, supporting organizations, and constituents around the country was aimed at holding hearings to educate members of Congress, demonstrate broad public support, and generate publicity.

The first hearing was held on March 19, 1976, in a House Ways and Means Committee, chaired by James A. Burke of Massachussetts. Ad hoc hearings were convened in March, 1982, by Ron Dellums, then a senior member of the House Armed Services Committee. In 1988, NCPTF submitted written testimony (supported by sixteen co-signing organizations) to the Ways and Means Subcommittee on IRS Oversight regarding the "frivolous tax penalty." This testimony noted that adoption of Peace Tax Fund legislation "would alleviate a persistent burden on the IRS while permitting those few but undeterrable citizens to pay their full share of tax without violation of religious conscience."

On May 21, 1992, the Ways and Means Subcommittee on Select Revenue Measures, chaired by Charles Rangel, held impressive hearings on H.R. 1870, the then-current U.S. Peace Tax Fund Bill. Mark Hatfield, chief sponsor of the Senate bill, S. 689, was the lead-off witness, followed by three House members: Andy Jacobs, lead House sponsor; Nancy Pelosi, Calif.; and John Conyers, Mich. Mainline Catholic, Protestant, and Jewish leaders also testified. Of the extensive oral and written testimony presented to that hearing, one example is that of Bishop Thomas Gumbleton, Auxiliary Bishop of the Roman Catholic Diocese of Detroit, and a founder of Pax Christi USA. Bishop Gumbleton said

> Many who cannot in good conscience participate in the military also find it morally unacceptable, on the basis of their conscience, to contribute to the military through the payment of taxes. The question remains of how to balance the legitimate right of the State to collect taxes for the common good and the equally legitimate right of those who, for religious or moral reasons, cannot contribute to military spending without violating their conscience. We believe that the U.S. Peace Tax Fund Bill

moves us toward resolving these tensions. While upholding the rights of the State to collect taxes and the obligation of citizens to contribute their fair share, this bill will also make it easier for those whose conscience will not allow them to contribute to the military nevertheless to fulfill their obligations as citizens.[3]

In 1995, Senator Hatfield, then chair of the Senate Appropriations Committee, sought a hearing on S. 1663, the Peace Tax Fund Bill. Senator Orrin Hatch of Utah, chair of the Finance Committee's Subcommittee on Taxation, indicated his interest in the bill based on religious freedom principles, but the hearings were never held.

The list of organizational sponsors of the Peace Tax Fund Bill grew from the nucleus of the historic peace churches to mainline religious groups and secular peace and civil liberties organizations, including local governments. Currently the NCPTF lists more than one hundred-eighty national and local groups.

The role of staff

Behind all of these events are the staff of the NCPTF, to which Marian Franz gave special leadership from September 1982, to December 2005. NCPTF staff, active committee members, and like-minded organizations have a Herculean task:

- on Capitol Hill: to get more congressional sponsors, to listen to suggestions from members of Congress and their staff and consider whether to incorporate them or find ways to answer their concerns, to get hearings and favorable witnesses to testify;

- at the grassroots: to motivate supporters around the country to lobby their representatives in Congress and be active in their local communities, to organize annual legislative briefings and lobbying days in Washington for supporters, to develop Congressional District Contacts, to work with a legislative committee of representatives from like-minded organizations;

- to find additional organizations which will support the Peace Tax Fund Bill, to speak to their leaders and assemblies;

- to publish newsletters, maintain a website, raise an annual budget, hire staff, and develop and support a governing board and officers;

• and finally to initiate, develop, and support awareness of conscientious objectors and taxes for war in other countries and at the UN.

What about the future?

We are fortunate that Peace Tax Fund Bill sponsors in the House have moved into key leadership roles. In 2009, Charles Rangel is chair of the House Ways and Means Committee. John Lewis is chair of that committee's Subcommittee on Oversight. Nancy Pelosi is Speaker of the House, and John Conyers is chair of the Judiciary Committee.

But based on the experience of the preceding decades, it seems clear that presidential leadership, or at least acceptance of the peace tax fund concept, is essential. Only then can IRS opposition be stilled and majorities achieved in the House and Senate. It was General Lewis B. Hershey and others before World War II who overrode congressional opposition and put the CO provision in the draft law. What is needed is a president who is sensitive to the First Amendment's protection of freedom of religion and to minority rights. Barack Obama has taught constitutional law and has been a member of the Congressional Black Caucus. Perhaps in an Obama administration, such leadership will be forthcoming, and the Religious Freedom Peace Tax Fund Bill might finally be enacted.

In 1962, Edward F. Snyder began serving as executive secretary of the Friends Committee on National Legislation in Washington, D.C. He served in this role until 1990, with a term as Quaker International Affairs Representative in Southeast Asia, stationed in Singapore, from 1967 to 1969. He worked on legislative issues with Marian Franz from the time she was hired by NCPTF until his retirement in 1990. He currently heads the Friends Committee on Maine Public Policy.

---

1. For a more detailed presentation of the courts' views regarding conscientious objectors' filing of cases seeking recognition of their right not to be forced to pay for war and military expenditures, see for example *U.S. v. Lee*, U.S. Supreme Court, 1982; and *Jenkins v. Commissioner of IRS*, Second Circuit Court of Appeals, March 6, 2007.

2. Each Congress begins in odd numbered years and lasts two years. Legislation does not carry over to the next Congress, hence the need to introduce new bills with a new list of sponsors every two years. Thomas, the Library of Congress web site, carries the bill number and names of sponsors for all bills since 1973, and the text of all bills since 1989 (*www.thomas.loc.gov*).

3. Testimony in *Congressional Record*, Serial 102-98, pp. 1-295.

Conscientious Objection to Military Taxation as a Human Right

Derek Brett

Why talk about a *right* of conscientious objection to military taxation? After all, many war tax resisters are content just to refuse to pay, thus denying governments the funds they need to sustain their military adventures.

One reason is moral. Many persons who are reluctant to pay for war are unwilling to take upon themselves the decision to break the law, even when they can see very clearly that the immediate effects of doing so will be beneficial. They see a great danger in doing anything to support the idea that everyone can choose to obey only laws with which they are in agreement. The exercise of a recognised human right, by contrast, cannot in itself be incompatible with the rule of law.

The other reason is practical. When we argue that we have a *human right* of conscientious objection to paying taxes which are used for military expenditure,[1] we do not need to convince anyone that it is *right* to object to such taxes—that paying for military expenditure is wrong. Of course it is wonderful when our arguments persuade others to share our reasons for objecting, but by the time we have converted enough people to make any difference, we should be well on the way to doing away with military expenditure altogether!

All we are asking is that those who have such an objection should be free to act in accordance with their consciences. In this we should have the support of all who uphold human rights, irrespective of whether or not they personally share the objection, or even disagree with it. The argument about conscientious objection can thus be won before the argument about military expenditure, opening up the prospect that, for instance through peace tax fund legislation, we can make sure that our own tax dollars are permanently diverted from military expenditure, rather than simply withheld until the tax authorities inexorably catch up with us.

So how to achieve recognition of this right? It is of course possible to petition "cold" for a new human rights instrument which might create it, but such a route is full of pitfalls. It is far safer to make out the case that the right is already implicit in what has already been "universally" accepted.

On December 10, 2008, the world celebrated the sixtieth anniversary of the adoption, by the General Assembly of the United Nations, of the Universal Declaration of Human Rights. Of course the Universal Declaration did not invent the rights it codified. But although its language is in many respects much more radical and forthright than anything that might be negotiated today, it has nominally been accepted by all members of the UN. That is what gives it its unique authority.

The Universal Declaration made no mention of conscientious objection. But this does not mean that it excludes it. Article 18 states (in the gender-insensitive language of the time): "Everyone has the right to freedom of thought, conscience and religion; this right includes freedom to change his religion or belief, and freedom, either alone or in community with others and in pubic or private, to manifest his religion or belief in teaching, practice, worship and observance."

Three points are worth noting here. First, the word order places the emphasis firmly on the belief system of the individual, not the hierarchy of organized religion. Second, there may be no mention of conscientious objection, but the underlying concept of conscience is included. Third, the definition is expanded to make clear that it includes not just what one believes but also the right to "manifest" that belief. In all these respects, the Universal Declaration is more powerful—and promising—than the more venerable First Amendment to the U.S. Constitution. Our crucial task, therefore, is to establish that conscientious objection, including conscientious objection to military taxation, is a "manifestation" of religion or belief within the terms of the Universal Declaration, a concept which "may include not only ceremonial acts but also such customs as the observance of dietary regulations, the wearing of distinctive clothing or head coverings, participation in rituals associated with certain stages of life, and the use of a particular language customarily spoken by a group."[2]

As soon as the Universal Declaration was adopted, arduous negotiations began at the UN to enshrine its provisions in a binding international treaty. Throughout the negotiations, a handful of non-governmental organisations (NGOs), with intermittent support from some governments, lobbied tirelessly for the inclusion of a specific reference to the right of conscientious objection to military service. (None were at that time working within the UN on the taxation aspect.)

The International Covenant on Civil and Political Rights (ICCPR) was finally adopted in 1966, but it did not enter into force for another ten years, as it first had to be ratified by thirty-five states (i.e. nations). Its Article 18 closely follows the wording of Article 18 of the Universal Declaration, and three further paragraphs are added; these do not however include a paragraph covering conscientious objection.

NGOs working on the issue did not give up, however. Surprisingly, the breakthrough when it eventually came was not achieved anywhere in the process of codifying international human rights law but in the General Assembly, the main political forum of the United Nations. In 1978, Ghana proposed a resolution calling on member states to grant political asylum to the increasing number of young men fleeing South Africa to avoid conscription. In consultation with the Quaker UN Office, New York, the Ghanaian delegation was persuaded to refer (in what became General Assembly Resolution 33/165) to "conscientious objection to service in military or police forces used to enforce apartheid." In this way, after thirty years, the vital phrase had entered the UN lexicon, perhaps by the back door, but without a single vote against.

This was the key to further advances. In 1981, the UN Commission on Human Rights requested its subordinate expert body, the "Sub-Commission," to study the question of conscientious objection with particular reference to the implementation of Resolution 33/165. The resulting "Eide Mubanga-Chipoya Report" ultimately inspired a resolution of the Commission on Human Rights which called upon states to "recognize that conscientious objection to military service should be considered a legitimate exercise of the freedom of thought, conscience and religion."

At this point, the focus moves to the Human Rights Committee. It is surprising how many accounts of the history of this issue completely fail to distinguish the Human Rights Committee from the UN Commission on Human Rights. These two bodies have nothing in common except the similarity of their names.

The Commission on Human Rights was the political forum in which the member states of the United Nations discussed human rights issues. Its outputs, like those of the General Assembly or the Security Council, consisted of resolutions, passed, if necessary, by a majority vote of the states present, in the person of their ambassadors to the UN. In 2006, as part of the UN reform package introduced by Secretary-General Kofi Annan, the Commission on Human Rights was transformed into the Human Rights Council. Perhaps the new title will prove slightly less confusing.

The Human Rights Committee, by contrast, is a body set up under Articles 28 to 45 of the ICCPR to oversee the implementation of that Covenant. The Committee comprises eighteen independent experts, elected by the States Parties to the ICCPR. The Committee's outputs are authoritative expert opinions, generally arrived at by consensus; they are styled "observations" (on periodic reports from states), "views" (on communications regarding specific cases in states which have accepted a right of individual petition), and "General Comments," which give guidance on the interpretation of the ICCPR. General Comment No. 22, concerning Article 18 of the ICCPR, was issued in 1993 and included (in paragraph 11) the statement: "the right to refuse to perform military service (conscientious objection) . . . can be derived from article 18, inasmuch as the obligation to use lethal force may seriously conflict with the freedom of conscience and the right to manifest one's religion or belief."

This authoritative interpretation of the ICCPR was reinforced by further resolutions of the UN Commission on Human Rights, all agreed without a vote. Commission Resolution 1998/77 effectively closed this round of "standard-setting," bringing together all the different elements of previous resolutions (establishing that there should be no discrimination between conscientious objectors on the basis of their particular views; that decision-making bodies should be independent of the military; that any alternative service should be non-punitive and truly civilian in nature; etc.)[3]

All this progress was of course with specific reference to conscientious objection to military service. This does not however mean it was irrelevant to our purposes. For when one form of conscientious objection is introduced, the way is opened for the discussion of others. Guarding against this "opening of the floodgates," General Comment 22 had specifically referred to "the obligation to use lethal force." The implication is that where the issues involved are not a matter of life and death, it would be harder to make out a case for a right of conscientious objection. But of course in conscientious objection to military taxation and conscientious objection to military service, *what* is objected to is the same; it is just the directness of the link which is in question.

And indeed the elaboration of the standards in the UN Commission on Human Rights has made it clear that the right of conscientious objection to military service is not exhausted when the objector is excused from personally bearing arms. Indeed, the dichotomy between conscientious objection to military service and conscientious objection to military taxation is not always helpful. It is logical to argue that paying taxes used for military expenditure is simply a different way of providing military service; that paying for war is a form of participation in war.

The closest the tax aspect ever came to a breakthrough was also in 1993, not in the United Nations, but in the European Union. A draft resolution appended to a report on conscientious objection prepared for the European Parliament by Juan Maria Bandrés Molet (Spain) and Rosy Bindi (Italy) contained a paragraph saying that the Parliament "considers that this fundamental right of conscientious objection also relates to tax contributions and calls therefore on the Member States to draw up a reply to the conscientious objections of people who are forced to support the military system through the national budget." The Christian Democrat group however voted as a bloc to ensure that this clause was *not* in the resolution approved by the European Parliament, on January 19, 1994. Although this was the fourth resolution of the European Parliament on conscientious objection within eleven years, the Parliament has not since returned to the issue.

The elaboration of standards is one matter; their conversion into "hard law" of the sort that courts and other judicial tribunals will follow is quite another. In fact it was not until 2004 that the Human Rights Committee was given the opportunity, by a carefully introduced case (to be accurate, two linked individual cases) from South Korea, to confirm that nations are obliged to consider the claims of those asserting a right of conscientious objection to military service, whether or not those nations have legislation on the subject. The two objectors were Jehovah's Witnesses—there could be no argument about the sincerity of their conscientious objection. The two, like hundreds of others each year, had suffered severe harm, having been subjected to automatic eighteen-month prison sentences for refusing military service. The only grounds on which the Committee could have found against them was if it were to say that it was entirely within the authority of a state to deny *any* right of conscientious objection. Such an interpretation was supported by only one member of the Committee, in a minority opinion, when the Committee's "View" was published in January, 2007. The remainder agreed a) that there had in these cases been

a violation of Article 18, Paragraph 1 of the ICCPR (i.e. of the freedom
of thought, conscience, and religion of the two Jehovah's Witnesses)
because the Republic of Korea had not shown the reasons for limiting
that freedom to be consistent with those permitted under the ICCPR; b)
that the state was obliged to provide compensation; and c) that it must
avoid similar violations in future.

The right of conscientious objection has still to be independently
confirmed under the *regional* human rights treaties, even though Article
9 of the European Convention on Human Rights and Fundamental
Freedoms (ECHR) and Article 12 of the American Convention on
Human Rights are again almost identical to Article 18 of the ICCPR.
It would have seemed that the European Court of Human Rights had
already had a clearcut opportunity to make such a ruling in the case of
Osman Murat Ülke, a Turkish conscientious objector who had spent
years in and out of military prison—every time he was released he was
called up again to perform military service; when he refused he was
court-martialled for disobeying orders—and who was now living in a
state of what the Court itself described as "civil death," unable to obtain
valid identity documents, to travel, even to register his marriage because
he had not performed military service. However, having decided that he
had clearly suffered from a violation of the article prohibiting "torture
or inhuman or degrading treatment or punishment," the Court decided
in January 2006 that it was not necessary to consider whether his freedom of thought, conscience, and religion had also been violated.

The jurisprudence under the American Convention on Human
Rights is even worse. In 2005, deciding a case from Chile, in which as it
happened no physical harm had been suffered by the complainants, the
Inter-American Commission on Human Rights had ruled that there was
at that time no obligation in international law requiring a state to recogn-
ise conscientious objection to military service. Paradoxically, in the same
Inter-American system, later in the same year a "friendly settlement" was
mediated under which not only did Bolivia agree to introduce conscientious objection legislation (it has not yet honored this undertaking), but
also to exonerate the complainant—a Jehovah's Witness—not only from
military service but also from the tax usually levied in lieu of such service from those exempted. While a very exciting precedent in practice,
this was not a court ruling, so it has no bearing on the law.

By contrast to the slow standard-setting work with regard to conscientious objection to military service,[4] attempts to argue that there is a right

of conscientious objection to military taxation were in fact first made through the judicial process, by cases invoking the First Amendment of the U.S. Constitution in the U.S.A., Article 9 of the ECHR before the European Court of Human Rights, and Article 18 of the ICCPR before the Human Rights Committee. The most frequently cited case under the ECHR is *C v. United Kingdom*, which was submitted in 1983; it however never reached the European Court of Human Rights itself, being declared inadmissible in pre-screening. That precedent has never been overturned. The issue was brought to the Human Rights Committee in 1991, in the case recorded as *J.P. v. Canada*.

In its decision on admissibility, issued shortly before General Comment 22, the Committee agreed that "article 18 of the Covenant certainly protects the right to hold, express and disseminate opinions and convictions, including conscientious objection to military activities and expenditures." It was *not* however ready to give serious consideration to a tax objection case, and declared it inadmissible with the words "clearly falls outside the scope of protection of this article." A case from the Netherlands which had been lodged shortly afterwards was disposed of with reference to this admissibility decision. In the autumn of 1993, a new case from Germany invited the Committee to reconsider their reasoning in *J.P. v. Canada*. It was in fact ruled out on a technicality, but the Committee added an observation that they would have seen no cause to depart from their previous reasoning.

At this point the international judicial route had obviously stalled. In retrospect, all these cases were premature, representing as they did attempts to enforce a right which had not yet been widely accepted. This is where Marian Franz came to the rescue. Through her work in the legislative arena with the National Campaign for a Peace Tax Fund, Marian appreciated the importance of slow and patient lobbying, gradually working on the climate of opinion until it had shifted. She saw the necessity for the same "persistent voice" also to be heard at the international level, mirroring the years of diligent work which had gone into the progress on the recognition of conscientious objection to military service.

Marian was therefore a prime mover in the decision made at the 1994 International Conference on War Tax Resistance and Peace Tax Campaigns to create an international NGO, Conscience and Peace Tax International (CPTI), to work on the issue. In 1997 it was Marian who made the presentation to the UN in New York which obtained "consultative status" for CPTI. Since then, in New York and Geneva, CPTI has been among the NGOs working on issues of freedom of religion and conscientious objection, and by its very presence (and its name), CPTI has been a constant reminder of the issue of conscientious objection to military taxation.

Where do we go from here? For the moment it is clear that none of the international judicial bodies is yet ready to rule that there is a right of conscientious objection to military taxation. The first necessity is to consolidate the jurisprudence that conscientious objection to military service is a human right. The hope is that the favorable decision in the case of the South Korean Jehovah's Witnesses can be the foundation stone of a gradually broadening body of legal and quasi-legal precedent. Already, in July 2008, the UN's Working Group on Arbitrary Detention used that decision to state (with regard to Turkish conscientious objector Halil Savda) that in the absence of legislation accommodating conscientious objectors, *any* imprisonment of a genuine conscientious objector for the refusal of military service could constitute arbitrary detention. In the past, they had ruled that the repeated imprisonment of conscientious objectors in Turkey and Israel for their refusal of military service amounted to repeated punishment for the same crime. South Korea itself is still stalling on the introduction of a proposed alternative service; the Human Rights Committee should soon have an opportunity to extend their previous decision to other South Korean conscientious objectors of various different beliefs.

Colombia is another country with no legal provisions recognizing conscientious objection to military service. The conscientious objectors in Colombia are being encouraged to bring to the Human Rights Committee the next clear-cut case of forcible or other involuntary recruitment of a declared conscientious objector, so that the Committee has the chance to apply the logic of the Korean decision. A decision of the Committee is not a binding precedent for the Inter-American Commission on Human Rights but has persuasive force and would make it very hard for that body to follow its dubious Chilean decision in deciding any future cases from the region.

As far as the European system is concerned, a number of strong cases have already been lodged with the European Court of Human Rights by Jehovah's Witnesses from Turkey and Armenia, at least one of them citing *only* Article 9 of the European Convention on Human Rights, to force the Court to confront the central issue. We must hope that one of these cases is decided before the European Court comes to give substantive consideration to the case of the "Peace Tax Seven."

The Peace Tax Seven are war tax objectors from England and Wales, who brought a joint case through the English courts for judicial review under the U.K.'s Human Rights Act of 1998, which incorporated the European Convention on Human Rights directly into British law. Sitting in the Appeal Court, three Law Lords conceded that the European jurisprudence based on *C v. U.K.* might be worthy of reconsideration. But they did not feel that any British court was empowered to correct it. So the momentum of their case has brought the Seven to the European Court of Human Rights, as though the U.K. Act had never existed. In January 2007, they joined a queue of over one hundred thousand cases just waiting to be declared admissible. The delay is however not all bad news. Success in this case would represent an enormous breakthrough, but so far the European Court has not even been ready to concede a right of conscientious objection to military service. Far better it should have bitten that bullet before it is invited to take the radical further step of extending the principle to military taxation.

And in the corridors of the UN? We may have to keep patiently plugging away for another decade before the issue of conscientious objection to military taxation benefits from a breakthrough equivalent to the "CO apartheid" resolution, to bring it into the mainstream of the human rights dialogue. Or the breakthrough may be just around the corner. At the time of this writing, 2008, a new angle of approach to the UN, which might just do the trick, is being discussed in the U.S. It is still too soon to say, and that particular story is not yet ready to be told.

Derek Brett is originally from Britain but since 1993 has been based in Geneva, Switzerland, where his wife Rachel covers human rights and refugee issues for the Quaker United Nations Office. At different times he has been a geographer, a university administrator, and a Quaker Meeting House warden. Since 2002 he has represented Conscience and Peace Tax International at the United Nations in Geneva.

---

1. "Military taxation," although a convenient shorthand, is not actually an accurate description. There are countries in the world which have specific taxes earmarked for, and sometimes collected by, the military. Establishing a right of conscientious objection to such taxes may well be the first step, but it will not directly help most

objectors, who are faced with the situation in which part of the general tax revenue is applied to military expenditure.

2. Human Rights Committee, General Comment No. 22: The right to freedom of thought, conscience and religion (Art. 18): July 30, 1993 (UN Document CCPR/C/21/Rev.1/Add.4), paragraph 4.

3. For the full text of Resolution 1998/77 and the relevant paragraph of General Comment 22 see Emily Miles, *A Conscientious Objector's Guide to the UN Human Rights System* (London: War Resisters International CONCODOC Project, 2000, in collaboration with the Quaker United Nations Office, Geneva), which is also a useful source of reference on the system as a whole.

4. For a fuller account than that given here see Rachel Brett, "Persistent Objectors at the United Nations," in *The Friends Quarterly* (published by The Friend, London, UK) 35/7 (July 2007): 301-309.

Christians and the Payment of Taxes Used for War

WILLARD M. SWARTLEY

Of all the moral dilemmas that Christians wrestle with these days, paying taxes that underwrite war, such as in Iraq and in Vietnam forty years ago, heads the list of vexing issues. How do we live with the inconsistency of praying for peace but paying for war? I am grateful for Marian Franz's many years of outstanding leadership in urging government officials to support the Peace Tax Fund Bill. She headed up the National Campaign for a Peace Tax Fund with never-flagging enthusiasm, making courageous contacts with senators and representatives and educating us in our churches and educational institutions. She did a remarkable job. I always looked forward to, and was helped much by, her visits to and speeches at the Associated Mennonite Biblical Seminary. Over the years I wrote numerous letters to IRS and government officials urging them to support the then-current bill for the Peace Tax Fund.

In a recent book chapter on this topic, I treat at length four New Testament (NT) texts that are often read as authorizing tax payment.[1] Did Jesus or Paul instruct us to pay taxes, context and circumstances notwithstanding? The three Gospel texts are either irrelevant—Matthew 17:24-27 refers to a temple tax, mandated in Exodus 30:13, and so used in Jesus' time—or ambiguous. Mark 12:13-17 (with parallel in Matthew 22:15-22) has been interpreted numerous ways.

The third Gospel text, Luke 23:2, lists the Jewish charges against Jesus as they turn him over to Pilate for disturbing the peace. One of those charges was that he teaches people not to pay taxes. The Jewish leaders want to make Jesus appear as a Zealot, but Luke has Pilate clearing Jesus of this and other charges (chapter 23). Nonetheless, an analogous "false witness" charge in Mark 14:58 that Jesus threatened to destroy the temple is not without foundation. Jesus' cleansing of the temple (Mark 11:15-18) and his statements on the occasion (John 2:19-21) were interpreted to support that charge. Similarly, Jesus' brilliant response to his

57

"tax testers" in Mark 12:15b-17 was also interpreted as support against tax payment, rightly or wrongly. Both these cases contain irony. They are presented as "false testimony," but at the same time the Gospels show Jesus critical of the governing powers (see the gospel texts in column 1 in my chart on NT views of the powers).[2]

The fourth text is from Paul, Romans 13:6-7. This is the only text that instructs believers to pay their taxes. However, Paul's instruction was likely influenced by the current popularity of a tax revolt. The text refers to two types of tax: the poll tax (*phoros*) and an indirect commission tax (*telos*). The latter ignited the revolt, and Paul's instruction is conditioned by not wanting Christian believers to be hunted down for joining the commission tax revolt, especially in view of the fact that eight years earlier (A.D. 49) emperor Claudius had expelled Jews from Rome (and likely Christians too, since many were Jewish). Paul wanted the gospel to spread and the church in Rome to grow. When the historical-political context as well as the literary context of Romans 12:1–13:10 are assessed, caution arises against making a "pay all tax" application of this text to our current situation.[3] The literary context calls us to not be conformed to this world's evils (12:1-2), to not repay evil for evil (12:17), to live peaceably with all people (12:18), to leave vengeance to God (12:19), to feed your hungry enemies and give them drink (12:20), to overcome evil with good (12:21), and to owe no one anything, except to love one another (13:8). In light of these clear commands, we do well to ask, how can we pray for peace, and yet pay for war?

After examining these texts, I conclude:

> [W]e must be careful that we do not simply adopt the position of the Pharisees, that law is the final word on moral issues. Significantly, Jesus' reply points beyond the rights of the emperor to the rights of God. God's claim and the emperor's claims must never be put on the same level. The text may not be interpreted in such a way as to equalize God's and Caesar's rights. As Donald Kaufman rightly says, "Jesus' view of life implies a reservation in regard to the state but none in regard to God. For [Jesus] there was never any doubt that God was supreme even in the realm which Caesar claimed for himself."[4]

What guidance, therefore, does this text give to the question of paying taxes used for war? First, in view of the hypocritical and accusing intent of the questioners as well as the cryptic nature of Jesus' response, we acknowledge that Jesus and the opponents of Jesus hold differing views on this sensitive issue. Second, we do not allow ourselves to take the Pharisees' side in making law the sole judge of moral obligation. Finally, we see clearly that Jesus' answer does not tell us to give Caesar whatever he asks for.[5]

From text to present[6]

Romans 13:6-7 gives no indication that the moral issue, the use of tax monies to support Rome's military and political oppression (the so-called *Pax Romana*[7]), entered into Paul's consideration. Nor do the secular sources from that time period connect the tax revolt to a protest of Rome's military policies, but rather to an onerous commission tax, recently imposed. In other words, Paul is not asked nor does he answer the question: "What is the Christian moral obligation regarding tax payment when the tax is used mostly for military defense and war?"

One might argue that Paul does answer the question (and, by this analysis, answers it in support of paying military taxes) by his categorical statement in Romans 13:6-7, because he knew (from his extensive travels) that the poll tax financed Rome's military presence throughout the empire. But to deduce this answer from Romans13:6-7 parallels the argument used in the 1800s that Paul endorses slavery as an institution because he prescribes Christian conduct for slaves and masters. In both cases Paul was regulating Christian response to systemic conditions in a non-democratic society in which believers in Rome had no right to protest. In the larger literary context of Romans 12–13, Paul describes the Christian ethical motivation and action that is normative even in the face of this situation. It is essential that we take historical and literary contexts into account, to guard against misuse of Scripture.

Wider biblical considerations

In finding biblical directive on any moral issue, it is imperative to consider the entire biblical witness on a given issue. The following ten strands of biblical teaching bear on this particular moral issue of paying taxes that are used for war purposes:

1. The Decalogue's sixth commandment, "You shall not kill" (Exodus 20:13, Revised Standard Version), means that it is God's prerogative to take life, not ours. As a disciple of Jesus Christ, I cannot kill or approve killing one for whom Christ died. Wilma Bailey in her 2005

book[8] has persuasively shown that the Hebrew word here (*tirtsakh*, from root *ratsakh*) more likely means "kill," not "murder," as in the New Revised Standard Version (NRSV). Her conclusion is based on a contextual study of the thirteen uses of the word in the Old Testament (OT). The change to "murder" in the NRSV is unwarranted. If we object to killing in war, should we not be consistent and refuse tax that supports preparation to execute war?

2. The OT prophets, beginning with Moses, called for trust in the Lord as the true and adequate defense. They criticized the buildup and use of military power. Isaiah 2 and Micah 4 speak of beating "swords into plowshares." Further, Isaiah 2:6–3:17 condemns Israel for its idolatries: running after other gods and relying on military might. For these, judgment comes. Paying taxes to finance war aids and abets this idolatry.

3. The OT gives examples of those who refused to obey the orders of kings:

   • The Hebrew midwives: Shiphrah and Puah (Exodus 1:5-22)

   • Moses' mother and Pharaoh's daughter (Exodus 1:22; 2:10)

   • Daniel and Esther (refer to these books)

   • Jeremiah, in speaking against the king's policies, and counseling subjection to God's imminent judgment through enemy invasion.

4. Jesus commanded, "Love your enemies and pray for those who persecute you." Also, he said, "Blessed are the peacemakers." Jesus linked both of these commands to being "children of God." (Matthew 5:9, 44-48). Peacemaking is thus the identity mark of God's children.

5. Jesus said, "Give therefore to the emperor the things that are the emperor's, and to God the things that are God's" (Matthew 22:21). The two are not equal. What we owe to God stands above and before what we owe to the state, as the quoted verse also implies.

6. Jesus, even as king, repudiated domination over others, refused use of the sword for self-protection, and chose the way of the cross. In the NT we are called to imitate Jesus in this regard.

7. Both Daniel's and the apostles' testimonies concur with this model: "We must obey God rather than any human authority" (Acts 5:29).

8. The NT epistles speak of God as "God of peace" eight times. Nowhere in the NT is God designated "God of war." This bold innovation from Paul's writings is most significant.[9]

9. The church, composed of former enemy peoples, is now at peace in one Christ-body. This peace-union, God's new creation in Christ Jesus, manifests to the principalities and powers the manifold wisdom of God (Ephesians 3:9-10). This "mystery" of God's wisdom is jeopardized when we support war that results in "Christians" in one nation killing "Christians" in another nation.

10. Jesus' lordship extends over both the church and the powers (Colossians 2:10, 15).[10]

Appropriation to current challenge

How then should peacemaking Christians in the United States respond to the war-tax dilemma? On one hand Romans 13:6-7 can be cited in support of paying all taxes. On the other hand, the moral imperatives (in the literary context of Romans 12–13) of nonconformity to the world's values, living peaceably with all people, love for all, seeking to overcome evil with good, and concern for the worldwide missionary cause raise major reservations, and for some of us, a decisive directive not to pay taxes used for war.[11]

To be sure, for those Christians who see Paul's command to be subject to the authorities as requiring participation in military service, this topic is not an issue. They would accommodate it with just-war rationale. But this study supports those who have understood the Bible to forbid the Christian's participation in war. What is at stake in the holding of these different positions, with both appealing to Scripture, are several crucial principles of biblical interpretation. We give priority to the NT over the OT, thus relegating Israel's practices of warfare to a level of non-normative morality. But as recognized above, the OT also bears witness to resisting the authority of governmental powers when it conflicts with God's will. On moral issues, the life and teachings of Jesus are central for moral guidance. Further, Paul's specific counsel to "be subject" to the authorities does not mean indiscriminate obedience. When given only these two alternatives, Christians committed to Jesus' peacemaking commands are thus called to disobey government rather than participate in the military.

On the issue of tax payment specifically, we answer *yes* in principle, but *no* if that response violates the moral principles that in Romans 12-13 frame Paul's specific counsel in 13:6-7. Similarly, we violate basic biblical principles of morality when we use Romans 13:7 indiscriminately to support payment of taxes used for war. When we do that, we use Paul's specific counsel to legitimate a practice that repudiates the basic moral principles out of which the specific counsel arose. The difference between the historical cultural situations and the issues addressed account for this problem. Changed circumstances and questions call for different specific counsels. The basic moral principles remain the same. For example, the basic principle behind holy war in the OT is trust in Yahweh, a principle that carries through into the NT; but God's commands to fight against enemies cease with Jesus' command to love the enemy, and with the early church's redefining the boundaries of God's peoplehood (Ephesians 2:11-22; Colossians 3:11). Changed historical realities together with unfolding revelation from the OT to the NT necessitate new moral considerations. If that were not so, Jesus Christ's coming would be superfluous. The salvation encounter with Christ would not mean any moral change.

Personal response to the issue

In an effort to follow the basic moral principles of the NT of Romans 12–13—do not be conformed to the world, live peaceably with all people, owe nothing but love, overcome evil with good, submit to governmental authority and promote the missionary cause of the gospel—I have resisted payment of a percentage of my annual tax. Mary (my spouse) and I do this as a form of witness. In this resistance to tax payment we are not against paying taxes in principle, since we support government taxation to provide health, education, and social services to the poor, disabled, retired, and even universal health-cost coverage. We believe this witness accords with the gospel of peace, trust in God, and the way of love.

We've written letters to the Internal Revenue Service, our representative and senators, and the House Ways and Means Committee about this. Our resistance has taken the form of writing a second check, payable to Public Health Service (formerly Health, Education, and Welfare) equal to the percentage of our taxes which are allocated to military expenditures. (Earlier, this second check was one-third of the total tax, excluding Social Security, but now the 2008-09 federal budget allocates 45%-60% for defense and war-related expenditures, hence this second check will need to be a higher percentage if we have tax to pay in spring 2009.)

We ask the IRS to forward the PHS check in an envelope we enclose, addressed and stamped. Two times the amount actually went to a specific public health organization via IRS forwarding the check to PHS, and PHS allocating it to a specific need.

One Monday morning we received a surprise phone call from St. Elizabeth's Hospital in Bethesda, Maryland. The woman calling us thanked us for our generous contribution to the hospital (of which we knew nothing), and informed us that they were using it to improve services for their senior longer-term residents in the hospital. However, several years later the IRS levied our bank account and collected the amount sent to PHS for at least one of the two times the check was sent to PHS. Thus, in principle, the IRS did not accept the earlier check to PHS as a bona fide tax payment. In most years the IRS has simply endorsed and cashed both checks.

Our hope and prayer is that the witness given through the letters and phone conversations accompanying such action speak a word faithful to the gospel and also sensitize others to kingdom values and the gospel's critique of national priorities. We welcome Christian discernment and counsel to test this way of Christian faithful response to God's peace for humans.

Why support the Peace Tax Fund?

Although Mary and I have not made our second tax check payable to the National Campaign for a Peace Tax Fund, we have supported it regularly in contributions through the years. We have also contacted key representatives and senators, as well as ours in Indiana, to support the Peace Tax Fund Bill. As I reviewed these letters, the points of rationale for the Peace Tax Fund are: conscientious objection to war (as a member of the Mennonite church, one of the historic peace churches) and therefore opposition to participating in and paying for war; the huge budget for war and development of weapons is morally wrong and not a prudent use of tax dollars; to amass weapons capable of wiping out the world population numerous times over is morally evil, contradicting the teachings of Jesus; the Christian ethic calls us to love our enemies, seeking to transform enmity into friendship; our country is in desperate need of reordering budget priorities; moral prudence calls for caring for the poor in this country and around the world; and it is biblical to do those things that make for peace and do them through peaceful means (James 3:18). Our country needs a Department of Peace to develop peacemaking initiatives, inform diplomatic efforts, and counter the image abroad of the U.S. as a war-threatening/making empire.

We urge support of the Peace Tax Fund since such a fund would provide a way for those opposed to war to willingly pay all their tax and to underwrite numerous peacebuilding projects in the U.S. and around the world. The image of our country abroad would be vastly improved. Further, such projects would point the way to resolving conflicts peacefully (combined with diplomacy, modeling Carter's post-presidential role), even preventing many of the conflicts by giving bread not bombs, hope not hell (Eisenhower, "war is hell"), and love not hate. Though I have not put this in letters to government officials, such a fund could also underwrite, through a percentage amount of its total accumulation, whatever program emerges to provide universal health care coverage, though the big share of those funds must come through overall allocation of the annual U.S. budget, reducing military budgets and keeping our country out of wars that extend American domination of the world (most evident in the current war in Iraq, with the projected cost to the tune of *three trillion* dollars.)

We laud those who have given their lives and leadership to developing and promoting the Peace Tax Fund. On this occasion the accolades go especially to Marian Franz, unfailing and buoyant witness to the vision of a better way and world, in which the kingdom of God, manifest in Jesus Christ, comes nearer—as we pray daily in the Lord's Prayer.

Willard M. Swartley is professor emeritus of New Testament at the Associated Mennonite Biblical Seminary, Elkhart, Indiana. Among the many books and articles he has published are two on peacemaking: Covenant of Peace: The Missing Peace in New Testament Theology and Ethics *(Eerdmans, 2006)—a scholarly study of peace/peacemaking in the New Testament—and* Send Forth Your Light: A Vision for Peace, Mission, and Worship *(Herald Press, 2007), which includes an extensive study of the tax texts in the New Testament and the moral basis for tax resistance.*

---

1. Willard M. Swartley, *Send Forth Your Light: A Vision for Peace, Mission, and Worship* (Scottdale, Pa.: Herald Press, 2007), 129-151.

2. Willard M. Swartley, *Covenant of Peace: The Missing Peace in New Testament Theology and Ethics* (Grand Rapids: Eerdmans, 2006), 229.

3. *Send Forth Your Light*, 140-47; and *Covenant of Peace*, 236-40.

4. Donald D. Kaufman, *What Belongs to Caesar? A Discussion on the Christian Response to Payment of War Taxes* (Scottdale, Pa.: Herald Press, 1969; rev. ed., Eugene, Ore.: Wipf & Stock, 2006), 41-42. See further Kaufman's excellent discussion of these various texts, and especially his quotation of C. G. Rutenber on p. 41.

5. Swartley, *Send Forth Your Light*, 138.

6. This section is taken, with modification, from *Send Forth Your Light*, 147-51.

7. For the oppressive nature of the Pax Romana and the NT church's witness against it, see Swartley, *Covenant of Peace*, 38-40, 154-55, 164-70, 245-53; 421-23.

8. Wilma Bailey, "You Shall Not Kill" or "You Shall not Murder"? *The Assault on a Biblical Text* (Collegeville, Minn.: Liturgical Press, 2005).

9. Swartley, *Covenant of Peace*, 208-11, 258-59.

10. For a complete list of texts of Jesus' victory over the powers, see ibid, 229, the "Normative" column.

11. A helpful and important resource bringing together the voices of those opposing payment of taxes for war is Donald D. Kaufman's *The Tax Dilemma: Praying for Peace, Paying for War* (Scottdale, Pa.: Herald Press, 1978; reprinted, Eugene, Ore.: Wipf & Stock, 2006).

Part II

A Persistent Voice:
Selected Essays by Marian Franz

Yes, There is Another Way

Would you say that a $10,000 an hour wage was a good one? Suppose you had earned $10,000 an hour, twenty-four hours every day, including weekends and holidays since the birth of Christ. If you had made that amount every hour since Christ's birth, you would not yet have earned as much as this fiscal year's budget authority for new U.S. military spending, amounting to $253.6 billion. In fact, as your calculations will indicate, it would take centuries more before you would reach that amount!

The above is a graphic way to keep ourselves and others aware of the enormity of investments of money, time, energy, brains, and earth resources in death and destructive "security" and "peace."

> The nations have sunk in the pit that they made;
> in the net that they hid has their own foot been caught.
> —Psalm 9:15

The irony is that as the state loses its power to defend, its people identify more closely with it. We hear the paradoxical self-erasing argument, "Yes, I understand that we have more than enough to destroy any enemy, and ourselves in the process, but we must remain strong!" Those of us who work for passage of the World Peace Tax Fund Bill are helping to expose the myth. This is not peace or security. The emperor has no clothes.

The World Peace Tax Fund Bill is a well-crafted instrument. It can become a "conversation piece" for a variety of issues on the folly of the arms race. A soul search caused a Pentagon official to resign from his job, and he now works for peace. I asked him, when I was preparing a speech for a ministers' conference, what I should say. His reply: "Tell them what you've always told me. There is another way!"

A true prophetic pronouncement contains a *yes* and a *no*. No, we must not build weapons. Yes, we will pay our taxes plus above-budget amounts of time and energy for our nation's real security: conversion of suicidal military hardware into peaceful products that heal wounds. Yes, there is another way.

Going Where No One Wants to Go

A thought-provoking article, "The Abilene Paradox,"[1] tells of a group of four people on a 104-degree day, sitting on the porch in front of the fan, sipping lemonade, playing dominoes; each looking forward to an agreeable afternoon. "Let's drive to Abilene and have lunch," one suggested.

What, go to Abilene? Fifty-three miles? In this dust storm and brutal heat? And in an un-air-conditioned car? thought the second person. But not wanting to be the lone dissenter, he went along, "Sounds like a good idea." One by one the others supported the plan.

The trip was disagreeable, the meal unappetizing. Four hours and 106 miles later, they returned exhausted, covered with dust and perspiration. Irritated, they began to blame each other for the lost afternoon.

"I would rather have stayed here but went along because the three of you were so enthusiastic about going."

"I only suggested it because I thought you were bored."

To each one's surprise and shock, they learned that reasonable and educated adults had gone where individually and collectively they did not want to go.

I often wonder if the current arms race is a trip to Abilene. Could it be that with only a partial vision of potential disaster, each continues on the path on the false assumption that there is collective agreement, when in reality each secretly questions the validity and practicality of the plan?

The inability to manage agreement, not the inability to manage conflict, is the problem here. Members (of a family, organization, or country) fail to accurately communicate their desires and/or beliefs, thereby leading one another to misperceive the collective reality. The collective decision is therefore contrary to what they want to do, and the results are counterproductive to the group's intent, purpose, and interests.

The Watergate scandal called for agreement of many people to a pattern of behavior that later appeared stupid and reprehensible even to themselves. The central figures of the Watergate episode, high government officials, knew that for a variety of reasons the plan to bug the Watergate Hotel did not make sense. One after another they testified that they had qualms about the plans, but none stood up to say it should be stopped.

> SENATOR HOWARD BAKER: "If you were concerned because the action was known to you to be illegal, because you thought it improper and unethical, you thought the prospects for success were very meager, and you doubted the reliability of Mr. [G. Gordon] Liddy, what on earth would it have taken to decide against the plan?"

> JEB MAGRUDER: "Not very much, sir. I am sure that if I had fought vigorously against it, I think any of us could have had the plan canceled."[2]

Why then did no one stop it? The reasons: they felt a sense of loyalty; they feared loss of face, prestige, or position; and they feared ostracism as non-team players. When the illegality of the act surfaced, it was inevitable that blaming, self-protective actions, and scape-goating would result. The very ostracism that they had feared, and sought to prevent by going along, only compounded. The resultant disaster took on a scope and size that none could have envisioned. Each could have stopped it. Each, now humiliated, bore the responsibility for it.

Is the World Peace Tax Fund Bill a part of the way to locate the roadways that bypass Abilene? As we have explained our conscientious objection to military spending, we have helped others to confess their secret misgivings and to see the absurdity of plans which not only compound the very problems they are designed to solve but also defeat the purposes of the country.

Our challenge may not be to manage our conflict with the proponents of the arms race, but to manage our agreement. The power to destroy the Abilene paradox's ruinous influence comes from accurately speaking the truth and communicating our beliefs, and doing so in a manner which frees others to express theirs.

It takes a real team effort to go to Abilene ... Watergate ... Holocaust. It takes the courage of a relative few to stand up and stop it. We are the relative few. Our silence can be construed as consent. Our combined voice can steer us onto the Abilene bypass and save us from going where no one wants to go.

---

1. Article by Jerry Harvey in *Organizational Dynamics*, 1974.

2. "High Noon at the Hearings," *Time*, June 23, 1975.

A Ray of Light in the Darkness

It was a chilling experience to live through the Cuban missile crisis and to read, in retrospect, how very close we were to a nuclear confrontation with the Soviet Union. Especially vivid is the memory of putting my small children to bed at night. They were reluctant to sleep only because of their sheer exuberance for life and their impatience to delight in yet another day of discovery. I did not know if they would have another day. Beyond giving them the security of knowing that they are wrapped in a salvation that is beyond all harm, what does a parent say at such a time to these unblemished innocents in footed pajamas?

One of the factors that averted annihilation in 1962 was the moral intervention of Pope John XXIII. He appealed to each of the super-power leaders for restraint. Mr. Khruschev said at the time that that appeal had considerable weight on his thinking. In fact, he said, it was the first ray of light in the fast-developing darkness.

The political realists had failed. Why, then, did Pope John succeed? The shell of political determinism is, after all, supposedly impenetrable. Some decision-makers saw an obstructive evil. Some saw evil personi-fied in Mr. Khruschev. The Pope, however, refused to concede that there is any evil that cannot be pierced, and that there is any human being who cannot be touched. The most important cause on earth to Pope John was to make the planet fit for sacred humanity. In pursuit of this pur-pose he refused to believe that any doors were closed to him.

Admittedly, none of us has the stature and influence of this great religious leader. Yet we underestimate the weight we do have and the effect of our continued moral appeals through correspondence and especially through personal visits with members of Congress and their aides.

This does not mean that once the moral case is laid out, everything will conveniently fall into place. Minds are changed by repeated expo-sure to a new idea. Many of us work against increases in the military budget and against new (and old) weapons systems. When we focus on the World Peace Tax Fund Bill, however, we make a point that is unique: we focus on the individual's informed conscience. The mere fact of our existence and persistence gives repeated exposure to our convictions and causes legislators and their aides to run our message past their own consciences.

As night falls around the planet, people from a rich assortment of nationalities, cultures, and tribes put their children to bed, hoping only that their sleep will be peaceful and that their new day will be free of threat and danger. Gandhi said that almost anything you do will seem insignificant, but it is crucial that you do it.

The odds are intimidating. But what choice do we have, except to persist and insist that there is no evil that cannot be pierced; no person who cannot be touched? It is our light in the fast-developing darkness.

Converting Swords into Services

The architects of the Pentagon had a dream. They could not imagine, while designing it, that it would be needed as a military headquarters following World War II.

The Pentagon, built on land formerly called "Hell's Bottom," is a mile in circumference. It is a city within itself, providing office space for up to thirty thousand people on its eighteen miles of corridors. The building occupies 34 acres, surrounded by 67 acres of asphalt with parking space for 9,849 vehicles. An indoor shopping center in its concourse has enough room for cars to pass. Sixty thousand meals are served daily in the eighteen dining rooms. Built in a remarkably short sixteen months, the building was completed in 1943 at an approximate cost of $83 million.

Inside the Pentagon, one is constantly reminded of the architects' dream. In its rings, corridors, and bays, staff people do not move about on stairway and elevators but on broad ramps. Why ramps? After World War II this bastion of the military establishment would be converted into a greater center for healing—the ramps were designed for wheel chairs and stretchers! The Pentagon would be converted into a hospital—the biggest in the world, the best in the world.

The architects of the World Peace Tax Fund Bill had a dream. Some of the money in the World Peace Tax Fund would be used for "retraining of workers displaced by conversion from military production."

An example of such conversion and retraining is the Lucas Aerospace corporation in Great Britain, which employed fourteen thousand people on seventeen sites but threatened to shut down some of its facilities. Thousands of workers faced the threat of severe economic insecurity if they lost their jobs. Then something happened. Some of the workers devised a plan which solved their economic dilemma and proved that workers can design technology for beneficial rather then destructive purposes. In their "Alternative Corporate Plan" (six volumes of 200 pages each), the workers made an audit of the plant and their own skills. As a result, 150 products were designed with complete technical specifications in areas such as transport and braking systems, alternative energy

74

sources, and medical equipment. By designing their own industrial plan for the future, they prevented layoffs and converted their skills to developing 150 socially useful products.

It is a terrible thing when families feel that their economic security and well-being hinge upon continuation of an insane arms race. However, it is also a terrible dilemma for our legislators, who must try to reconcile responsibilities to the home district with what they perceive to be conflicting national interests.

As a nation we are dangerously close to (or past the point of) inventing new weapons just to keep people employed. Do votes to delete all funds for weapon systems fail because legislators are convinced the weapons are essential? Speaking of a recent vote, Representative Nicholas Mavroules, who authored one of several economic conversion bills, says, "No. I think they were worried that losing the MX [missile] would cost constituent jobs. But promotion of the arms race is a reckless way to give a guy a job. One computer error, one unidentified blip, one mistake could lead us to ruin in our hair-trigger world."

Not all munitions workers are pro-military. William Winpisinger, president of the International Association of Machinists and Aerospace Workers (IAM), the largest union representing defense workers in the U.S., says: "We need economic conversion programs so that one day those of us who depend upon military production for our livelihood can think about and act on war and peace issues, free from the fear of job loss and economic insecurity."

The people who are educating members of Congress and candidates for office about the provisions of the World Peace Tax Fund Bill have a dream. They realize that economic conversion is a cornerstone of reversing the arms race. They know that workers on military contracts must be retained for domestic production. That costs money, which the World Peace Tax Fund Bill would provide. That in itself is enough reason to support the bill.

The original plan to convert the Pentagon into a hospital was a huge and crucial effort to redirect a society, to re-align national priorities, to convert an economy. It did not happen—yet. But dreamers dream on. They know the truth of the Old Testament proverb: "Where there is no vision the people perish." They dream on of swords converted into healing—even at Hell's Bottom.

Where Were You When I Needed You?

During the awful days of the Vietnam War, a former member of Congress recalled the anguish of decision-making during his term in office as he tried to accommodate his own political interests, the economic needs of people in his home district, and the conflicting obligations of his own moral code.

He was privy, by virtue of his congressional committee assignment, to confidential briefings which revealed the extent to which the American people were being deceived about the conduct of the war. Totally repulsed by the killing and angered by the deception, he yearned to express his moral outrage. In his heart he had a speech ready to deliver with real passion on the floor of the House of Representatives. Not a word of that speech ever passed his lips or was expressed in a vote. Why?

There were several military installations in his home state. He assumed that the voters would not return him to office if he took an antiwar stand. Besides, he dreamed and planned about all the good he could do after the election, if only he remained silent now.

As it turned out, the voters did not return him to Congress. Enveloped in regret, he said, "How much better if I had at least gone out of office for a cause!" Soon after, he asked a question of a small group of us who were seeking meaningful ways to relate to legislators. His question still haunts me: "*Where were you when I needed you?* You should have hung in there with me. You should have urged me not to sell out!"

He continued, "I might not have paid any attention to you. I cannot promise that I would have listened to you at all. Nevertheless, you should have urged me to live up to my own highest good. You shouldn't have let me down."

As decision-makers are haunted by their silence, we too are haunted by ours. We share a duty.

Many considerations of political welfare, economics, feasibility, and other critical factors enter into the formal decision-making process that is carried out in hearings, staff studies, committee sessions, and on the House or Senate floor. Legislators deliberate—sometimes in loneliness, sometimes with a few trusted individuals in whom they have confidence.

Here there is a tremendous opportunity for us. Do you see it? It may be difficult to believe, but you can become one of those respected and trusted few. It is not that hard to do, if you are willing to do the homework and spend the time necessary to build the relationship. Many of you have already done so and have become a significant influence, as indicated by your thoughtful and vigorous correspondence and/or visits with your members of Congress.

In this role, we are relieved of the necessity of competing with Pentagon lobbyists who argue weapons technology, throw-weights, and mega-tonnage. Here we need to fully claim our own expertise and speak to the moral and ethical dimensions of decisions. Yet we must do so with a humility that recognizes the possible limitations of our own vision. Our nation's possession of, and expressed readiness to use, terrible weapons is for us a profoundly spiritual matter. We cannot remain silent.

When we are where we are needed (whether in or out of Washington), we are close enough to observe and nurture every leaning toward disarmament, to reinforce every instinct toward nonviolent solutions to international conflict, to beginning to expose every deception.

It is significant that our current strategy for the Peace Tax Fund Bill was suggested by a congressional cosponsor as he reflected on how his mind had been changed on issues. "What you need," he told us, "is to have six people in each congressional district who would continually keep the peace tax fund issue before their representative." He was not asking about a hit-and-run approach, of course, but one of patient and sustained encounter.

If you do not envision yourself in such a role, would you be willing to help name, appoint, and anoint six in your congressional district and/or state who would? Would you then support and encourage them in this critical task?

Decision-makers may listen to us—or they may not. Either way, we share responsibility for coming out of the silence.

Military Uniforms, Silk Suits, and True Believers

The positive congressional response to the revised Peace Tax Fund Bill has surprised me. Members of Congress who had objected to certain parts in the older version of the bill are reconsidering sponsorship; others are seriously looking at the bill for the first time. On a recent day, feeling light-hearted and energized as I do when things go well, I was quickly brought down to earth by the scene that surrounded me in a representative's outer office, although it was not unusual.

Three men in military uniforms, heavy with ribbons, appeared in the doorway for their congressional appointment. They dismissed the receptionist's invitation to be seated. They were not accustomed to waiting, and this day would not provide them with the opportunity to learn that skill. Within one minute they were ushered into the representative's office.

The Department of Defense is forbidden by law from having registered lobbyists. Yet it has personnel engaged in "legislative liaison" work. There are several hundred of them; they work full time. Some of them are in uniform and some are not. They seem omnipresent. Their generous salaries are paid by the taxpayers. The current request in the president's budget is $13.4 million for "legislative liaison" work for next year. (Compare that to the $19.4 million for the *entire* budget of the Arms Control and Disarmament Agency, or the $1 million which is allotted for the first year of the beleaguered Peace Institute.)

In the same office, waiting for appointments, were two men in silk suits holding leather briefcases, there to represent the interests of one of many of the nation's large businesses. Many large companies and organizations hire lobbyists or lawyers such as these to represent them in the full political process. Some of these "guns for hire," as they are called in Washington, are very powerful—more powerful at times than the representatives themselves. Some companies, literally household names because they make household products, have almost invisible appendages that build parts for weapons.

It occurred to me that the military uniforms and the silk suits in that room really represented the military-industrial complex in microcosm.

Each twin alone is a power giant. The interrelationship of the two, with interlocking directorates, forms the powerful combination that results in congressional disbursement of vast resources for military production and research. And thus the military-industrial complex extends its long reach of influence far into both domestic national priorities and American foreign policy.

The lobbyists in uniforms and silk suits would be listened to, I knew. After all, look at the economic and political rewards and reprisals they can offer and threaten for "right" and "wrong" votes. In the company of such overwhelming power, one feels rather intimidated and diminished, as I felt by the time I heard the "how are you?" of the aide whom I was to see.

"I feel like I am being squeezed between the Military and the Industrial and it is giving *me* a complex!" I replied.

He laughed, but took seriously my implicit question: What influence do we have when surrounded by such power giants? "Many groups like yours carry an entirely different kind of persuasive power," he said, "because they have their basis in a moral conviction about right and wrong—about the morality or immorality of a given policy."

He continued, "If the group is composed of 'true believers' who are focused on issues vitally important to them, and if they are deeply committed to their cause, that intensity of feeling can multiply the group's influence far beyond its numbers."

He's right, of course. We have all watched tiny seeds produce fragile shoots that displace the heavy hard-crusted earth. It matters that we deepen our faith. It matters that we become one with humanity that suffers because of our military priorities. The military-industrial-congressional dialogue need not be held without our input. We can articulate the meaning of conscientious objection and killing. Whether or not they understand it, they will know that it exists and that it will not go away.

Who is intimidated by vast power forces that would seem to forbid the sprouted seed from reaching the light? Not the true believers.

"Enemies": Foes Today
Can Be Friends Tomorrow

FALL 1985

It was a powerful lesson for a little girl to learn. During the years of World War II, there were German soldiers in the busy fields of my Kansas childhood home. No, they had not invaded that deeply into U.S. territory. These prisoners of war were billeted in a small nearby town, and were available to work on local farms during the day.

These "enemy" soldiers held no fear for me. What terrified me were the U.S. guards who accompanied them. They were the ones with the guns. In total terror I watched as one, upon being urged, demonstrated how to attach his bayonet for action. No gun intended to kill people or to spear stomachs had ever before been near our home.

At first, the guards were tense, the prisoners wary. At noontime on the first day, after washing up out-of-doors with the rest of the harvesters, they waited outside to be served. Perhaps the prisoners expected to be served out-of-doors from tin cans? My mother stepped onto the porch and, in perfect German, invited them in to her table as graciously as she would have any other guest. Overcome by the unexpected kindness, several wept.

As time passed, the tension between the German and the U.S. soldiers was eroded on both sides by the hospitality that our Mennonite home and community extended equally to friend and foe. Guards no longer brought their dreaded guns to the table (to my enormous relief!) but left them on the porch. After meals, we all gathered around the piano to sing hymns and folksongs in both German and English. These "enemies" who, in other circumstances, would have been shooting each other, swapped photos of and longings for their families back home. My father translated jokes they wanted to tell each other. These seemed to be mostly about war and military superiors.

One afternoon, to escape the broiling Kansas sun, the single guard for that day had gone to nap under the shady trees along the creek, leaving the prisoners alone with the farmers. Suddenly, excited chatter erupted amid a frantic flurry of activity. The prisoners had spied a fast-approaching army jeep with its cargo of military superiors coming to inspect the guard on duty. Several prisoners rushed to the creek to waken the guard, who hastily rubbed the sleep from his eyes and regained his watchful post. There were salutes, weapons inspection, some conversation.

Satisfied that the prisoners would not escape under such vigilant watch, the officers disappeared as quickly as they had arrived. The silent tension of the field broke into explosive laughter as guard and prisoner alike enjoyed the success of that close call.

What was a little girl to think? If the German and U.S. soldiers were not each other's enemies, who *was* the enemy in the war? Had these soldiers of fiercely warring countries not just made common case against the real enemy—the system of war?

"Enemies," I have since noted, come and go with considerable speed. In the past half century, Germany, Japan, and China have turned from being our country's friend to foe and back again. The Soviet Union reversed that cycle: foe, friend, foe. Exaggerated fear of Soviet "enemies" is used to create disproportionate Pentagon budgets and provide defense contracts for large corporations. Yet, as opportunities for trade present themselves, the "enemy" diminishes. Those who would inflate our fears do not seem as afraid of the "enemy" as they want us to be.

It is rewarding to read copies of your letters to Congress and note that *you* are not thermometers that automatically rise and fall with every manipulation of popular hatreds. Rather, your expressions of conscience serve as thermostats, which help to moderate the irrational fears that take potential friends to the brink of death.

There is a way to multiply your good individual efforts. That way is explained in an article titled "Delegations of Conscience," by Ruth Flower, chair of NCPTF's Legislative Committee, which appears elsewhere in this issue. Won't you please read, re-read, digest, duplicate, distribute, discuss, and (if it seems right to you) carry out the suggestions in "Delegation of Conscience?"

Deep Commitment Communicates

Their three-minute appointment with the president stretched into nearly half an hour. On that January day in 1940, as war was fast approaching, President Roosevelt shook hands with each person in the seven-member delegation of "historic peace churches" (Mennonite, Brethren, Quaker). He asked some of the delegation about a project that they were engaged in—resettling European refugees and outlining various types of alternative service for conscientious objectors in case of war. Three years earlier, on a similar visit, a letter presented by one of the church groups had read as follows:

> We wish to assert again our patriotism and wholehearted loyalty to our country, even now as we appear before you to state our inability, on the grounds of our conscience and religious conviction, to participate in war or military service of any type. As a matter of record now, we humbly state to our Government that, before God and our conscience, we cannot assume responsibilities or services, the purpose and end of which is the destruction of human life.

Now, in 1940, the president assured the delegation that he understood and respected their work with resettling refugees and their position. "I am glad you have done it. That's getting down to the practical basis. It shows us what work conscientious objectors can do without fighting. Excellent! Excellent!"

Hearings on the conscription bill, which would establish alternative service for drafted conscientious objectors, were held a few months later, with testimony presented by a wide variety of religious and civil liberties organizations. A majority of the members of Congress were unsympathetic and hostile, expressing few concerns about the rights of conscientious objectors, but with barbed questions attacking the validity of the position of conscientious objection itself.

When the dust settled, the bill in its final form was changed to include the peace churches' demand for alternative service under civilian direction. Absent, however, was any provision for the non-religious conscientious objector, which supporters of the conscientious objector provision had also championed. Congress feared that dropping the religious test would open the floodgates (sound familiar?) to communists seeking to evade their responsibility. Despite formidable odds, the bill was passed that 1940 summer, due largely to the backing of a popular and powerful president.

At a press conference following the event, someone is said to have commented to Selective Service Director General Hershey, "You surely have to admire the peace churches for their will power." His response: "I don't know about their will power, but they certainly have a lot of won't power!"

In examining those early statements, one does not find the word *won't*. Ninety-year old H.A. Fast, who has persevered in interpreting to the government the conscientious objector position during and between five U.S. wars, expresses it another way, "It's not that we won't. We can't."

Pacifism is not taken seriously in the United States Congress. Pacifists, however, sometimes are. That is why we at the national office of the NCPTF make trip after stubborn trip to Capitol Hill. We do it to support your "I can't" message. The task of extending the conscientious objector provision to include "alternate service" for tax dollars is politically monumental. The moral case, however, is strong. But we can never reproduce or replace the eloquence with which you express your own deep convictions in letters and visits to your members of Congress. Deep commitment communicates.

We Are Not Alone

We are not alone. Peace tax campaigns—alive and well—exist in a number of other countries. Is that fact of significance to us? Yes. It will help us in Washington and it will help you in your local districts. To lobby effectively for the Peace Tax Fund Bill, one has to explain what conscientious objection really is. The difference between conscientious objection and mere disagreement with government policy is hard for many public officials to grasp. Being able to point to conscientious objectors all over the world and noting that others share our struggle in a variety of government settings help us to make that distinction.

I wish you could have been with me to attend the first International Conference on War Tax Resistance and Peace Tax Campaigns in Tübingen, Germany, in September. One hundred participants from thirteen countries accepted the invitation to attend. The purpose of this first conference was not only to provide first-time, first-hand contact but also to establish a structure to ensure continuing information exchange and international cooperation.

The political, ethical, and religious backgrounds of the participants varied. There was little diversity, however, in their resolve to address the untenable situation in which they found themselves: having to make wars possible through the taxes they pay.

The mood of the conference was serious and intense—sometimes grave. From the Tübingen church where we met, we could see a hospital for brain-damaged persons from World War II, now under conversion into a training center for the triage method of treating the victims of the next war!

Many of the participants had experienced war first hand. Those too young to have known World War II had felt its severe effects on their families. Susumu Ishitani, peace tax representative from Japan, was in Nagasaki when the bomb fell, and related its horrors. The Chernobyl nuclear accident had affected some conference participants directly and personally, creating anxiety. The majority felt insult and outrage at Pershing II and cruise missiles being planted by the U.S. in Europe. The depth of this feeling is too little understood in the United States. All shared a *grosser angst* (great fear) of those national policies which continue to shorten the nuclear fuse.

I have visited a number of Third World countries and have become accustomed to being sent back to Washington with a clear message for my government about how U.S. policies adversely affect segments of their populations. But I was surprised to find myself being sent home with the same kind of heavy message from Europe. "We're glad you came," several persons told me. "We have been helped by watching you in the United States and how you dealt with the civil rights movement, the Vietnam years, and the women's movement, as well as your peace tax campaign. But now it is time for you to learn from us." And they are right. We would do well to beware the mistakes of the Hitler years, when it gradually became too late too protest. We would also do well to learn from the positive qualities of European nationalism, where they do not share the U.S. bipolar view of the world.

Together in Tübingen we were witnessing the birth of a new international network. Together we were experiencing also both the joys and challenges that attend a new birth. We returned home strengthened by what we had learned from each other and by the knowledge that we are not alone.

Conscientious Objectors' Self-Defense

Conscientious objectors are to be commended—even admired—runs a familiar observation, but their naive optimism cannot be shared by more responsible citizens. "I must commend you for the integrity of your convictions and can certainly understand your opposition to the use of your tax monies for military purposes. However, while I am sympathetic, I must remind you that we do not live in the age of innocence. . . ."

This recognition of personal conscience has some value, but it carries the implication that any minority stands on grounds of conscience against war and preparation for war are to be dismissed by realists as a kind of deviant and morally eccentric position. Another inference is that we conscientious objectors are irresponsible idealists who sit back passively because of a personal distaste for war. We are therefore urged to pay-in-full for what is euphemistically called "national defense."

Our conscientious objection, however, is not something for which we wish to apologize. Our task is to show that conscientious objection should be celebrated! And we must not tire as we go about this task! Why is it so important to articulate and re-articulate, interpret and re-interpret, the dictates of conscience as we experience them? Ponder these words:

> Why, of course people don't want war. Why should [someone] on a farm want to risk his life in a war when the best he can get out of it is to come back to his farm in one piece? Naturally the common people don't want war: neither in Russia, nor in England, nor for that matter in Germany. That is understood. But after all, it is the leaders of a country who determine the policy, and it is always a simple matter to drag the people along, whether it is a democracy, or a fascist dictatorship, or a parliament, or a communist dictatorship. Voice or no voice, the people can always be brought to the bidding of the leaders. That is easy. All you have to do is tell them they are being attacked, and denounce the pacifists for lack of patriotism and exposing the country to danger. It works the same in any country.[1]

These words were spoken by Hermann Goering, commander of Hitler's Air Force, in his jail cell during the Nuremberg Trials which followed World War II. Around the same time, but thousands of miles away in San Francisco where he was attending the conference that founded the UN, the future President John F. Kennedy wrote to a friend: "Wars will exist until that distant day when the conscientious objector enjoys the same reputation and prestige that the warrior does today."[2]

Are Goering and Kennedy right? Is it easier to wage war when pacifists and conscientious objectors are defamed and dismissed? If so, it is time for conscientious objectors to engage in their own self-defense. How does one give verbal expression to feelings of conscience that go deeper than words?

The right to conscientious objection, based on deeply held religious and moral grounds, is an urgent issue, yet the discussion of it can quickly slip into an exchange of stereotypes, leading to a stalemate in communication—or worse. With this issue of the newsletter we conclude a more helpful four-part series by Dick Blackburn on conflict resolution skills related to the lobbying dialogue. By popular demand, this series is being reprinted in pamphlet form.

We now initiate a new emphasis for the Campaign: to help one another to give expression to what conscience really is. It is a serious and significant challenge. We will struggle to make it clear that, far from being a negative concept, conscientious objection to war springs from a very positive inner source and issues in positive peacemaking. We invite you to join us. Have you read or written moving expressions of conscience such as excellent letters, speeches, court statements, etc.? If so, would you send them in so that we can share them more broadly? We need everything from high-sounding phrases to simple expressions of the heart. You can then use these, together with the Blackburn articles, to help you talk with others about conscientious objection without estranging them, to bring them along with you until they can truly hear—and experience for themselves—your heartfelt convictions.

Our individual expressions help the collective conscience to come to life. They make that "distant day" of which President Kennedy spoke less distant.

---

1. Gustave Gilbert, *Nuremburg Diary* (Cambridge, Mass.: De Capo Press, 1995), pp. 278-279.

2. Arthur M. Schlesinger Jr., *A Thousand Days: John F. Kennedy in the White House* (Boston: Houghton Mifflin, 1965), p. 88.

Lest We Lose Our Conscience

Hear these stirring words: "Our sole safeguard against the very real danger of a reversion to barbarism is the kind of morality which compels the individual conscience, be the group right or wrong. The individual conscience against the atomic bomb? Yes. There is no other way."

I found these rousing words on conscience in the editorial of the August 20, 1945, issue of *Life* magazine, the first issue of *Life* after Hiroshima changed the world's life expectancy for all time. In contrast to earlier issues that began to depict life in the United States returning to normal with a war winding down, the August 20 issue explodes with horror and shock. Full-page pictures show Hiroshima "before" and "after." Articles scream: "The Atom Bomb: Its First Explosion Opens a New Era," "Hiroshima: Atom Bomb No. 1 Obliterated it—Nagasaki: Atom Bomb No. 2 Disemboweled It!" The editorial adds: "The thing for us to fear today is not the atom but the nature of man, lest he lose either his conscience or his humility before the inherent mystery of all things."

We do well to note that consciences and humility *do* get lost. Nations lose theirs. So do individuals. Our own consciences—once tender and compelling—can without proper nurturing dissipate into a thin serum which, failing to fever us, actually inoculates us against the jolt of passion and compassion which the editors of *Life* felt when first beholding the horrors of the atomic bomb. Conscience and humility are linked. Conscience dulled can decompose into a brittle self-righteousness.

Lest we lose our conscience: We need to keep our own conscience freshly fueled and deeply rooted by basing it on a cycle of deep reflection and action. A live conscience thus nurtured is continually tender to the point of pain. It is sensitive always to those who are the victims of violence and national policies that marginalize certain segments of humanity. A live conscience is politically independent. "An independent movement of conscience whose cry for justice and peace is rooted in the Bible rather than political ideology is the hardest to discredit, ignore, or accuse of communist sympathies," says Jim Wallis of the Sojourners community.

Lest we lose our conscience: Allow yourself to be stirred by expressions of other "believers." Conscience is contagious. The search for truth joins us with many others in the search for truth, and for genuine solutions. Listen to individuals whose conscience allows them no other choice than to decline to pay the military portion of their taxes. It is not that they *will not* but that they *cannot* pay that portion of their taxes which is used for military expenditures. Read the statements of a growing number of religious bodies who have decided, or are debating, whether they as a corporate entity can any longer withhold taxes from the salaries of employees who ask that those not be withheld for reasons of conscience.

Lest we lose our conscience: Remember that the Peace Tax Fund Bill opens the door for dialogue on what conscience really is and how it operates in our lives. It upholds respect for individual conscience as a civil liberties measure, and outlines positive peace-enhancing uses for redirected tax monies. The aide of a member of Congress crucial to the movement of the Peace Tax Fund Bill said: "After hearing your expressions of conscience I view the bill differently than I did before. Keep talking about conscience. Once you stray from conscience, you're lost!"

Lest we lose our conscience: keep the emphasis on hope. Life based on conscience is a real possibility. Reawakened individual consciences can animate the conscience of a nation and lead the change beyond our dreams. It has happened before in the abolitionist, women's suffrage, and civil rights movements. It can happen again.

To prevent the death of all things, we dare not to lose our consciences or our humility before the inherent mystery of all things. The individual conscience against the might of the military-industrial complex? Yes. There is no other way.

Conscience, the Goad

On a grave marker in an old English cemetery are these words:

> Conscience needs no persuader;
> But is of itself the goad;
> It brooks no pain, regret or grief;
> One step, then all is well.

One wonders, when contemplating such a headstone, who lies beneath it. What manner of life, what manner of death, would have occasioned such an epitaph?

Conscience needs no persuader . . ."In the depths of his conscience, man detects a law which he does not impose upon himself, but which holds him to obedience. Always summoning him to love good and avoid evil, the voice of conscience can when necessary speak to his heart more specifically: do this, shun that" (Pope John XXIII, Second Vatican Council).

But is of itself the goad . . . Conscientious objectors are "those whose consciences, spurred by deeply held moral, ethical, or religious beliefs, would give them no rest or peace if they allowed themselves to become any part of an instrument of war" (U.S. Supreme Court in *Welsh v. U.S.*, 1970).

One Step . . . "The push, the push of conscience is a terrible thing," said one person whose one-step-at-time struggle with conscience led him eventually to prison. Others have said, "It is not the fear of physical death in the trenches that has led to our remaining in prison, but rather fear of spiritual death," and "if we kept forever on this side of the line, we would die within ourselves."

Then all is well . . . "After agonizing for years, I felt a burden had been lifted. The experience of jail can be extremely dehumanizing," said another person, "but for me, it was an experience of freedom, freedom from the fears that had immobilized me and shackled my conscience."

These statements can help us interpret to members of Congress and to fellow citizens the place and function of conscience in our own lives. Conscience is a non-negotiable goad.

I found a quite different definition of conscience in an old volume in the Library of Congress: "Conscience is that part of the human individual which is soluble in alcohol." The writer goes on to say that conscience is removable and alterable by brainwashing. Unfortunately that belief is still held by many. Haven't we all heard the suggestion that a simple readjustment of our logic would solve our dilemma over taxes for military force? "Why don't you tell yourself that all of your money is going to good causes and that it is the tax dollars of others that will be used for war and preparation for war?" Poof, your problem is gone.

But neither toying with our logic nor alcohol spares us the wrenching dilemma. Neither of these "solutions" gives conscientious objectors any "rest or peace." Conscience needs no persuader. Many present day conscientious objectors declare, as did Martin Luther at his tribunal, "Here I stand. I can do no other."

Legal Losses, Moral Witness

Claus Felbinger's conscience would not abide by majority rule. Pleas by the religious hierarchy would not persuade him to recant. Nor did the State's chains, dungeons, racks, or threats of death. Here is how the sixteenth-century martyr responded to the contest between divine law and human law:

> Therefore we are gladly and willingly subject to the government for the Lord's sake, and in all just matters we will in no way oppose it. When, however, the government requires of us what is contrary to our faith and conscience—as swearing oaths and paying hangmans' dues—then we do not obey its command. This we do not out of obstinacy or pride, but only out of pure fear of God. For "it is our duty to obey God rather than men."[1]

Through the ages to the present moment, petitioners before courts have claimed the ultimate right of conscience: not to participate in the intentional killing of another human being. And through the ages those in the dock seem to bring the state itself to trial. Legal losses do not prevent forceful moral witness that rouses other weak consciences that would otherwise tend to yield to majority opinion. During the past decade conscience has been tried before numerous courts, each testing various constitutional amendments.

Anthony v. Commissioner of IRS (1978): Robert Anthony, a Quaker, argued that forcing him to pay for war was the same as forcing him to shoot a gun. This, he said, interfered with his worship as a Quaker, because worship included living pacifism as a way of life. Not to live as a pacifist would force him to accept a form of worship foreign to his conviction. Anthony was denied.

Graves v. Commissioner of IRS (1979): Bruce and Ruth Graves followed Anthony in 1979 and based their case on the free-exercise clause also. They argued that constitutional right takes precedence over an IRS regulation and that "only the gravest abuses endangering paramount interests give occasion for permissible limitation" of the free exercise of religion. The court denied the claim.

The Rev. Howard Lull, an Episcopal priest; his wife, Barbara; and Peter Herby, a Roman Catholic peace activist; brought the Ninth Amendment argument to the Supreme Court in 1980. They argued that the retained rights under that amendment prohibit the government from subversion of conscience. The early Christian church, they said, "forbade the receipt of money for magistrates polluted by war." Case denied.

Charles Purvis v. Commissioner of Internal Revenue (1981) argued concerning the violations of international law under many treaties to which the United States is signatory concerning wars of mass destruction. Purvis established that he was caught on the horns of a dilemma—either he would be in violation of international law by paying his war taxes, or by not paying his war taxes he would be punishable under the domestic law. The Supreme Court denied his claim also.

The Supreme Court in 1973 reviewed a landmark case in which a federal judge had ruled that the first amendment right to free exercise of religion was violated by forcing the American Friends Service Committee to withhold taxes from conscientious objector employee salaries. The Supreme Court reversed the lower court decisions. That reversal however, was based on a technicality, not on the constitutional question.

Despite seemingly strong constitutional and international law support, conscientious objectors have been repeatedly defeated in their court battles against military taxes. Some have therefore presented Congress with the Peace Tax Fund Bill. They consider it advisable to work on enlarging statuary protection, rather than depending on the courts and the constitution.

Conscientious objectors continue to be dragged into court. Courts continue to decree that we must pay for killing of the innocent. Conscience continues to say "*No.*"

---

1. From Claus Felbinger's Confession of Faith, addressed to the Council of Landshut, Bavaria, in 1560.

This Train is Bound for . . .

Franz Jägerstätter's conscience had its own unseen commander and would salute no other. Not Hitler. Not religious leaders. Not well-meaning friends. This Austrian farmer could not be budged from his conscientious refusal to serve in the army. Priests, and even Jägerstätter's own bishop, joined authorities in urging compliance with law. "This is a war of self-defense, and self-defense is always an exception to violence. It is not your place to decide whether the war is just or unjust," they pled. "Besides, your individual refusal to serve will make no difference to the Nazi war machine." Franz Jägerstätter, the father of three young children, weighed the costs of obeying and disobeying conscience. He found the cost of disobedience too high. He was beheaded in Berlin in 1943. Shortly before his execution, Jägerstätter wrote about a dream:

> I saw a beautiful shining railroad train that circled around a mountain. Streams of children—and adults as well—rushed toward the train and could not be held back. I would rather not say how many adults did not join the ride. Then I heard a voice say to me: "This train is going to hell."[1]

For Jägerstätter the train symbolized the whole Nazi system. He refused to board the train to hell.

Acts and words of conscience such as these are not motivated by any particular government, party, or ideology. It is the victims and potential victims of violence which compel the conscience. The sole aim of conscience-prompted words and actions is to prevent bloodshed and human suffering.

We, too, have our shining train. Several times a year a "White Train" laden with a cargo of freshly assembled nuclear weapons makes its slow journey from the Pantex plant in Texas to ports on either coast. Our train transports the instruments of hell.

For twenty years the White Train traveled unnoticed and unhindered. Then people stirred by conscience began to hold vigils and press conferences in towns along the tracks. Some towns now prohibit the train from

94

going through their vicinity. The white cars of the train have since been repainted other colors. The train has been re-routed to avoid vigilers. New punishments for those interfering include criminal penalties and fines up to $100,000. Nothing silences conscience. The people continue to appear along the new routes.

We must respect the fact that conscience draws the line for each of us in a different place. But each does find an area we dare not trespass. To cross the line is to board the train to hell.

Conscience prevents many from paying that portion of their income taxes which fuels the shining train. They weigh the cost of obeying conscience: audits, garnishes, court appearances, possible property loss, and even imprisonment. The cost is high, but how high the cost of disobeying conscience? What of the victims and potential victims?

Many of you continue to pay a price for your stand of conscience. Courts and even jail cells have become new pulpits for speaking clearly and convincingly about the train to hell. Such acts and words of conscience cause others to re-examine their own consciences.

Please remember how important it is that you share your own struggles. How can members of Congress have anything but a fractional understanding of this definition of conscience and its non-negotiable demands over our lives if we do not communicate? We are grateful for copies of your letters, and for accounts of the moving ways you tell your stories when you visit members of Congress personally.

There are intrinsic rewards for not boarding the train. The chaplain who visited Jägerstätter shortly before his execution said he would never forget the face: "It shone with such joy and confidence." Jägerstätter wrote, "Neither prison, nor chains, nor sentence of death . . . can rob a man of his faith and his free will . . . God gives so much strength that it is possible to bear any suffering, a strength far stronger than the might of the world."[2]

---

1. Gordon Charles Zahn, *In Solitary Witness: The Life and Death of Franz Jägerstätter* (Holt, Rinehart and Winston, 1965), p. 111.

2. Ibid. pp. 97, 233.

A Partnership in Conscience

For over six years I have represented our common concerns about conscience and taxes for military force in Washington, D.C. After hundreds of visits in House of Representatives and Senate offices, I must tell you something. I have never met "the Congress." I have never engaged in dialogue with "the state" or conversed with a policy. But I do meet people—just plain people. All of our theories and theologies—of church and state, of religious freedom and governance, of divine law and human law—are in the end all transmitted in a rather ordinary person-to-person encounter.

It's occasionally good to step back and focus some careful thought on the quality of that one-on-one relationship. To do so, we must consider the setting, how decisions are made, what means of communication will be effective, and what our manner communicates. The four best ways to humanize the process of getting to members of Congress, says former U.S. Representative Bob Edgar, a Peace Tax Fund Bill co-sponsor, are "eye contact, staff contact, telephone contact, and letter contact."

"The system doesn't work well unless a partnership is built," advises Edgar. "You've got to begin your lobbying effort back in your own home state, in your congressional district, and there build a one-on-one relationship."

"It is up to everybody to tell the dilemma and personal side of their own story," continues Edgar. "It is best to humanize the data. Those constituents most helpful sit one-on-one across the table, form coalitions, and personalize the problem. It is best when I get to know them as people, when they are accurate in the information they share, when they are clear in the way in which they think, and when they've brought one or two pieces of paper and keep my office posted."

In this relationship of conscience, we often underestimate the effect of our continued moral appeal through correspondence and especially through personal visits with members of Congress and their aides.

Thich Nhat Hanh, a Buddhist monk and activist, observes: "The peace movement can write very good protest letters, but they are not yet able to write a love letter. We need to learn to write a letter to the

Congress or the president of the United States that they will want to read and not just throw away."[1] "Love letters" foster open-minded questioning, non-judgmental moral witness, and offer ideas and information without preaching.

Agreed, voters do not always send the best and the brightest to Congress. But it does no good—actually, *worse* than no good—to assess blame and pronounce judgment. Blaming is an easy mode to fall into, particularly when we feel members of Congress are responsible for faulty national decisions. But blaming causes defensiveness, closes listening ears, and triggers the need to strike back. Conflict resolution skills help us to understand that it is better to be persuasive than argumentative or demanding. The challenge (not an easy one) is to fight *national* self-righteousness without *personal* self-righteousness.

Decisions on the moral and ethical aspects of issues are not made in congressional committees but deep within the legislators themselves. We must proclaim our own expertise on conscience and speak to the moral and ethical dimensions of congressional issues. Yet we must do so with a humility that recognizes the possible limitations of our own vision. One member of Congress, who was able for the first time to understand our concern of conscience, told me: "My mind was changed by those who did not polarize the debate on this issue into 'us' and 'them.' Instead, these people helped to transform my attitude because they helped me to see the facts and decide for myself without being made to feel like the enemy."

---

1. Thich Nhat Hanh, *Being Peace* (Berkeley, Calif.: Parallax Press, 2005), pp. 81-82.

When Conscience Stands Alone

J eanette Rankin, a committed and lifelong pacifist, is today celebrated for her uncompromising stand against U.S. entry into two world wars. Montana's early passage of the suffrage amendment enabled Ms. Rankin to be elected to Congress four years before the Nineteenth Amendment gave all women in the U.S. the right to vote in 1920.

Despite warnings that the suffragette movement would suffer and that she would not be returned to office, she voted her conscience, joining fifty others in voting against U.S. entry into World War I. "I want to stand by my country but I cannot vote for war," she declared. "I vote no!"[1] Newspapers called her a disgrace to womanhood and evidence that women were not yet capable of holding office. She was not re-elected for a second term in the House and was defeated in a subsequent bid for the Senate in 1919.

During World War I she witnessed the conflict between conscience and the law, as many conscientious objectors went to prison—some for nearly two decades. She understood the nature of conscience as a combination of intellectual and moral convictions, which are so deeply ingrained that the individual cannot recognize any temporal authority which attempts to impose a course inconsistent with those convictions.

Out of office, she lectured throughout the country on behalf of peace measures and neutrality legislation, proposed legislation against war profiteering, testified before the Senate committee investigating the munitions industry, and lobbied for the National Council for the Prevention of War. In Switzerland, with Jane Addams and an international gathering of wives, mothers, and sweethearts of World War I soldiers, she helped found the Women's International League for Peace and Freedom.

In 1941, she was returned to Congress by Montana constituents just in time for another pivotal vote. On December 8, 1941, the day after the Japanese attack on Pearl Harbor, Congress was again debating a declaration of war. Jeanette attempted to add to the debate her conviction that "the world must finally understand that we cannot settle disputes by eliminating human beings." Angry shouts of "Sit down!" Sit down!"

interrupted each attempt to speak. When her name was called for the vote, she stood and declared firmly, "I vote no! As a woman I cannot go to war and I refuse to send anyone else."[2] That vote ended her political career.

After the vote, Congresswoman Rankin ran into an anteroom and shut herself inside a telephone booth where she sobbed at the hatred that caused war and at the animosity directed at her. The reaction of the crowds to her vote of dissent was so riotous that police had to escort her across the street to her office. In that dark hour Ms. Rankin could not have known that one day her statue would stand in the U.S. Capitol to dignify that very House wing in which she had needed a police escort for her safety. On the pedestal would be the worlds she had just spoken, "I cannot vote for war."

In her remaining years she visited Gandhi and gave speeches all over the world. "I'm going to start with the young people. I must make them understand that here is no glory in war. They must learn to regard war as they do cannibalism . . . You can no more win a war than you can win an earthquake."[3] Pleading with youth to write members of Congress, she said, "Tell them to spend our taxes on homes, hospitals, schools."

My favorite quote from Ms. Rankin is this: "They that take the sword, shall perish by taxes." She was right. An arms race is itself an act of aggression. Some of our U.S. cities today look as though bombs have already fallen on them. "Every gun that is made, every warship launched, every rocket fired, signifies, in the final sense, a theft from those who hunger and are not fed, those who are cold and are not clothed," said Dwight Eisenhower.[4] Conscientious objectors are still penalized because they cannot pay that portion of their taxes which goes to eliminate human beings. They, too, stand alone. They *cannot* violate their convictions.

---

1. Hannah Josephson, *Jeannette Rankin, First Lady in Congress: A Biography* (Bobbs-Merrill, 1974), p. 76.

2. William Miller, as told to Frances Spatz Leighton, *Fishbait: The Memoirs of the Congressional Doorkeeper* (Prentice-Hall, 1977), p. 63.

3. Josephson, *Jeannette Rankin*, p. 135.

4. Dwight D. Eisenhower, Speech to American Society of Newspaper Editors, Washington, D.C., April 16, 1953.

John Woolman: Conscientious Objector in Colonial America

SUMMER **1990**

To refuse the active payment of a tax which our society generally paid was exceedingly disagreeable; but to do a thing contrary to my conscience appeared yet more dreadful.
                                                              –John Woolman[1]

J ohn Woolman, called the quietest radical in history, lived during the last half-century of the colonial American period (1720-1772). You may want to read John Woolman's journal, first published in 1774 and later edited by John Greenleaf Whittier, for insights and quotes as rich as those I've quoted here. The journal, or spiritual autobiography, was the characteristic literary expression of the time.

A lifelong New Jersey tailor, Woolman was a master of many trades, including the operation of a dry-goods shop. His retail trade "increased every year, and the way to large business appeared open." But the typical American economic pattern of expanding business operations was not Woolman's way. To better attend to "inward business, the true business of my life," he withdrew completely form his profitable retail trade. Truth, he said, required him to live "more free from outward cumbers" (91).

Numerous examples show that his philosophy on conscientious objection was based on being "so mixed in" with the mass of suffering humanity that he could not consider himself "as a distinct or separate being" (264). Once he was asked to write a bill of sale for a black slave. At a time when few religious people (white, that is) saw the injustice of slavery, his first-hand experience caused him to name it "a dark gloominess hanging over the land," whose consequences would be "grievous to posterity" (72). As the embers of the French and Indian War flamed in sporadic massacres, Woolman, unarmed, visited the Indians on the Pennsylvania frontier. He wrote, "Love was the first motion and thence a concern arose to spend some time with the Indians, that I might feel and understand their life and the spirit they live in" (192).

Woolman found the roots of war in economic greed and the lust for power. Customarily, he began with an inward search for the sources of evil. "May we look upon our treasures, the furniture of our houses, and our garments, and try whether the seeds of war have nourishment in these our possessions" (307).

Woolman's own words give the setting for this starkly dangerous and hate-filled time. "The calamities of war were increasing; the frontier inhabitants of Pennsylvania were frequently surprised; some were slain, and many taken captive by Indians; the corpse of one so slain was brought in a wagon, and taken through the streets of the city in his bloody garments, to alarm the people and rouse them to war" (128).

The dilemma for conscience was acute. When the recruiter came to town, some in the Quaker community informed him "that they could not bear arms for conscience' sake; nor could they hire any to go in their places, being resigned as to the event. . . . To refuse an active payment at such a time might be construed into an act of disloyalty, and appeared likely to displease the rulers, not only here but in England; still there was a scruple so fixed on the minds of many Friends that nothing moved it" (128-130).

Woolman's journal entry, "Considerations on the Payment of a Tax laid for Carrying on the War against the Indians," is dated 1757-1758.

> As scrupling to pay a tax on account of the application hath seldom been heard of heretofore, even amongst men of integrity, who have steadily borne their testimony against outward wars in their time . . . It equally concerned men in every age to take heed to their own spirits; and in comparing their situation with ours, to me it appears that there was less danger of their being infected with the spirit of this world, in paying such taxes, than is the case with us now. . . . I believed that there were some upright-hearted men who paid such taxes, yet could not see that their example was a sufficient reason for me to do so, while I believe that the spirit of truth required of me, as an individual, to suffer patiently the distress of goods, rather than pay actively. To refuse the active payment of a tax which our Society generally paid was exceedingly disagreeable; but to do a thing contrary to my conscience appeared yet more dreadful (125-126).

John Woolman's example deserves consideration if not emulation. Though his convictions led to unpopular actions, he set a standard for love in an era full of hate.

---

1. John Woolman, edited by John Greenleaf Whittier, *The Journal of John Woolman* (Boston, 1872), p. 125.

Choosing Targets

The USSR has, for many decades, been the target of our concentrated fears and of twelve thousand nuclear weapons. Profound and unanticipated changes have now eclipsed anxiety about our former antagonist and enemy. According to the polls, the U.S. citizenry has buried Cold War fears. The Russians aren't coming.

If that is the case, U.S. military spending is being reduced, right? We won't be making any more nuclear weapons, right? Wrong, on both counts. Military spending is going up, not down. The latest Pentagon budget is up $5 billion in 1992 alone—it will be up by $12 billion by 1996—and those figures don't include any of the additional costs of the war in Iraq.

Saying that Eastern Europe is no longer a "target-rich environment," The Pentagon struck about one thousand Eastern European nuclear targets from the U.S. war plan. In a dramatic television speech, President Bush announced the destruction of 2,150 land-based tactical nuclear weapons. However, that still leaves the U.S. with seventeen thousand nuclear weapons.

Build-down and build-up continue to co-exist. The Department of Defense is naming new targets and is seeking "improvements" in the accuracy of U.S. strategic weapons. It is arguing for a third generation of nuclear "earth-penetrating warheads." The new weapons will enable targeters to assign fewer warheads to achieve the same level of destruction. In addition, the B2 bomber is getting a fresh, hard sell (at the cost of nearly $1 billion per plane, it is already literally worth its weight in gold). And SDI, or Star Wars, now has an affectionate and endearing new name: "G-PALS" (Global Protection against Limited Strikes).

The current nuclear weapons complex includes fifteen major sites in thirteen states; spread over an area the size of Delaware, Rhode Island, and the District of Columbia combined; employing about one hundred thousand people. It has produced sixty thousand war heads. Health and environmental concerns, however, have prompted a not-in-my-back-yard attitude. In its Weapons Complex Reconfiguration Study, the Department of Energy is therefore proposing a new plan for the twenty-first century.

This plan, called "Complex 21," is designed to consolidate these sprawling locales into one or two "super bomb-building sites"—a nuclear weapons theme park, I suppose. Scheduled to be operational by 2015, the plan would commit funds for twenty-five years of construction. And while you've got your calculator on hand, add this: officials say the cost of cleaning up environmental damage at existing aging facilities is expected to be as much as 10 times greater than the cost of Complex 21.

The true cost of the Cold War, however, must be calculated not just in terms of trillions of dollars spent on the military, not just the commission of crimes against the environment, not just the enormity of the task of cleaning up the existing mess, not just the expense of repairing and restarting dilapidated bomb factories and the cost of building new facilities, not just the fact that there is no place to put additional radioactive waste. "The problem in defense," said President Eisenhower, "is how far you can go without destroying from within what you are trying to defend from without." The cost is also in terms of sacrifices made in health care, immunization of children, repaired roads and bridges, drug control and treatment, relief from debasing poverty, and education (our bombs are smarter than our kids). This policy makes war on life. The number of homeless people—in our country alone—enters the millions. Stomachs and spirits are empty, and despair produces soaring murder rates.

A look at military planning and its staggering costs is a stark reminder of what prompts the conscience—the present and potential human suffering caused by military expenditures. Conscience sees hungry children, the environment, health care, and poor countries as a target-rich environment for our energies and resources.

The weapons have boomeranged and the destruction intended for external targets has pierced us. In the end, our enmity has done more harm than our enemy.

Sojourner Truth:
A Witness for Conscience

Sojourner Truth knew first hand the cruelty of slavery. She bore on her body the marks of the whip's lash, and in her heart the pain of forced separation from her family, first from her parents and later from her children. Yet Sojourner refused the compliant role scripted for a slave. She spoke forcefully and at risk against slavery. In situations fraught with great danger, she was pointed in her arguments, biting in her wit, sharp in her attacks, yet always tender and deeply compassionate.

As I read now about Sojourner, I see her motivated by a triple need to speak: for the betterment of those enslaved, for the sake of her own conscience and integrity, and, not least, as a favor to those who did not want to hear her. "Children, I'm against slavery because I want to keep the white folks who hold slaves from getting sent to hell."[1]

She confronted her taunters without rancor or bitterness, fear, or timidity. That appeal to the better sentiments of white people, by shaming them or encouraging them or complimenting them fast converted Sojourner into one of the most popular orators of the time. She convinced many listeners of the rightness of her cause and won the respect, admiration, and friendship of some of the great figures of her time—Frederick Douglass, Harriet Beecher Stowe, Susan B. Anthony, Abraham Lincoln.

Some audiences responded with hysterical abuse and scorn. "Down with you! We think the 'niggers' have done enough! Stop your mouth! We will not hear you speak!" A heckler once shouted, "I care no more for your anti-slavery talk than I care for a flea bite!" Sojourner's response: "Maybe not, but the Lord willing, I'll keep you scratching!"[2]

Isn't it interesting we speak of conscience as bothering us—as though by flea bites? Statements of conscience do keep people scratching, even after attempts to flick or swat them away.

A senator once called me a "friendly pest." Now, isn't that an interesting choice of words? He went on to say that it is the friendly pests—those so committed to their cause that they return again and again—who change attitudes and policy. Perhaps "friendly pest" is the nicest compliment you or I can hope to receive.

Sometimes fleas must bite strategically and simultaneously. I remember the swarms that descended on the halls of Congress during the Vietnam War. First, there were swarms of students. Then came the swarm called "Parents Too," followed by a swarm called "Lawyers Too," then "Physicians for Social Responsibility," and all the rest. As one group was swatted away, another came in its place. There is no doubt about it—individual acts and words of conscience bring the collective conscience to life.

Current purveyors or sojourners of truth, speaking their consciences, insist that the payment of those taxes which are designed for weapons to kill other human beings is for them an action that their conscience finds morally abhorrent, an action which contradicts their deepest moral and spiritual values.

Our words of conscience must be motivated as Sojourner Truth's were: for the sake of the victims of military violence, for the sake of our own integrity and conscience, and for the sake of people who resist hearing what we have to say.

Sojourner Truth knew that being an effective agent of change meant being a good pest. One wears people down, or rather, wears down the obstacles to communication. She was a reminder of conscience for those who would wander away from what mattered. Sojourner Truth kept the nation scratching at a time when too many people were silent in the presence of unspeakable wrongs. Her obsessive passion for the cause was transmitted by a profound compassion for her reluctant hearers. We have much to learn from her.

---

1. Jacqueline Bernard, *Journey Toward Freedom: The Story of Sojourner Truth* (New York: Feminist Press, 1990), p. 159.

2. Maxine Block et. al., *Current Biography Yearbook, 1992* (New York: H.W. Wilson Company, 1992), p. 182.

The Day the Ways and Means Hearing Room Seemed Like "Church"

My first telephone call the morning after the hearing on the Peace Tax Fund Bill came from David Wildes who, as chief aide to Peace Tax Fund Bill lead sponsor Rep. Andrew Jacobs, had invested a great deal of time and energy in the hearing's preparation. He said Rep. Jacobs called the hearing the most moving and inspirational level of discourse he had heard in all of his eighteen years in Congress, with one possible exception during the Vietnam War. David added his own comment, "It was a little like being in church."

The Ways and Means hearing room with its high ceiling and expansive chandelier is grandiose, magnificent, even intimidating. In lieu of stained glass windows, there are photographs of former members looking down from lofty positions in poses that are self-assured, aristocratic, regal. Testifiers must look up to address members on a raised dais.

What made it seem like a religious service was the testimony to conscience. Consider some excerpts from these "sermons":

The Creator of the world has imprinted in the human heart an order which their conscience reveals to them and enjoins them to obey.
–*Bishop Thomas Gumbleton quoting from Pope John XXIII's encyclical,* Pacem in Terris

Spiritual values are real. They are not to be treated as incidental or expendable to fit the needs of the state. . . . God intends us to live in harmony with our most deeply held beliefs. . . . we who are conscientious objectors cannot deny the conscience within us short of renouncing the God we believe in.
–*Alan Eccleston, Quaker*

I believe I am called by my Creator to live nonviolently, "to act justly, to love constantly, and to walk humbly with my God" (Micah 6:8). If my religious denomination believes my response is faithful, why then does my government not allow me to make this witness without living with the daily fear and anxiety that accompanies this faith witness?
–*Patricia Washburn, Episcopalian*

We believe that war-making is morally wrong. The words "just" and "moral" and "right" cannot, in our view, ever be used to describe a war.
 —*Rabbi Philip Bentley, president, Jewish Peace Fellowship*

What we have been doing to those of our nation who are opposed to war on the grounds of conscience when we use their monies to wage war is a sin against them. When we ignore their requests for justice and they are forced by conscience to choose between personal integrity and inhospitable law, it is not they who sin, but we.
 —*Chaplain Nelson Stone, U.S. Army Reserve*

Some spoke of their religious body's support for war tax resisters and/or the Peace Tax Fund Bill. For example, in its written testimony the three million-member Presbyterian Church (USA) explained why that entire body recently endorsed the Peace Tax Fund Bill even after the end of the Cold War. The action was inspired by the distress experienced by one member, a missionary, whose taxes for warfare in Central America would have killed the very people whom he was working to save.

It was Chairperson Rep. Charles Rangel who closed the hearing with this challenge to the congregation:

Friends, you have raised the issue to the highest standard. Now we have the political job of educating a larger number of people. You will have to help us educate other members of Congress. . . . I would encourage you and the tens of thousands that support you to continue to contact your members, to share with them the same concern . . . in your own eloquent way. It is up to you to validate this good testimony and witness for conscience.

An inspirational "church" service is never an end in itself. It can serve to excite in us new energies that will enlarge and amplify the witness to conscience that no one else is making. There is a lot riding on our response.

The full proceedings of the hearing are printed in the Congressional Record, *Serial 102-98, pp. 1-295.*

Validating This Good Testimony

"How in the world did you manage to get a hearing on the Peace Tax Fund Bill?" a congressional staffer asked in a somewhat exasperated tone. "Good grief! Your bill has less than fifty co-sponsors. Other bills are denied a hearing even with nearly two hundred co-sponsors."

As I reflected on what led to this unlikely May hearing, I recalled the words of Representative Andrew Jacobs some years ago: "History and morality are on your side." It was the persistence of the true believers, who for two decades would not be still about their convictions. You interpreted and articulated the insistent voice of conscience in such a way that you invited others to consider its merit. Members of Congress began to understand that the issue of conscience and military taxes addresses not only public law but also a higher law. Yes, we lack quantity, but not quality.

With the hearing we have taken a major step forward. Endorsements for the Peace Tax Fund Bill are coming from a growing number of highly respected organizations. The printed official record of the hearing gives many people access to the powerful testimony and will long be treasured by those who champion religious freedom and cherish the value of individual conscience. The hearing has given the bill stature and visibility and provides us with new opportunities. Media coverage of the event included the Cable News Network, *The Wall Street Journal*, and *The Washington Post*. Numerous radio interviews and talk-show programs are using the hearing and the bill as a topic for discussion and have increased awareness of the issues of conscience and war.

Working on the Peace Tax Fund Bill is like being perpetually ready to board a train that has no announced schedule. We prepared for a hearing during each of the preceding five Congresses. When the long-sought opportunity presented itself we were not caught off-guard. Catholic, Jewish, and Protestant witnesses, taxpayers, and legal experts—all were ready to give eloquent testimony about the legitimate right of those who, for religious or moral reasons, cannot contribute to military spending without violating their deepest moral and religious beliefs.

Now we need to be prepared for the train's next unannounced arrival. The Peace Academy Bill, in 1984, passed as a rider on another bill, but only after it had a hearing. After their hearing the Peace Academy supporters did not relax but used the momentum to build broad-based support.

Our option now is to use or lose the gains we have made. Rep. Charles Rangel of New York, who chaired the hearing, was totally persuaded by the sincerity of those who testified and urges us now to validate this good testimony. In a recent letter he offered congratulations and a challenge. "Indeed, a major step has been taken. You have raised the issue to the highest standard . . . I commend you and others for your diligence and fervor . . . however, it is still crucial that you continue your efforts with all members of Congress. On an issue as controversial as this one, it is essential to gather broad-based support."

The three thousand letters you sent were presented in six large binders at the hearing. They are now in the library of the House Ways & Means Committee. Board member Rosa Packard of Connecticut has copies of the letters and is reading each with an eye to placing some in an abbreviated version of the hearing. Those letters do the most good on the desks of your members of Congress. Continue to write and mail such letters again. And again.

Letters should, as before, frankly state the religious/moral basis of your convictions. A witness for conscience that cites only political or social objections to U.S. foreign policy or misplaced national priorities misses the point. Mention the basic religious/moral convictions which motivate your life. In fact, an outline for your letters might be the three questions you will have to answer in essay form to qualify when the Peace Tax Fund Bill becomes law:

1. What is the nature of my belief about the participation in war?

2. How did I come to hold this belief?

3. How does this belief affect my life?

Ask your member of Congress to send you a copy of the hearing record. (*Congressional Record* Serial Number 102-98). Your representative may then become acquainted with the fact and content of the hearing. Quote from the record in your letters. You may also wish to state practical arguments. As they made the point that more revenue would be collected if the bill were law, Representative Jacobs and Senator Hatfield called this a "win-win" bill. Representative Jacobs teased that he should rename the Peace Tax Fund Bill the "Tax Revenue Enhancement Bill," to indicate that the government would collect more taxes through increased voluntary compliance and decreased collection costs.

I am told that it takes a hundred hammer blows on a Vermont marble cliff to show even the first tiny hairline fissure. Does that mean the thirty-seventh blow has no effect? The fifty-second? The seventy-fourth? Faith keeps us persistently hammering away even when there is no indication that our effort does any good. The marble cliffs of Capitol Hill are vulnerable too. If we didn't know it before, we know it now: No witness for conscience is ever lost!

Lucretia Mott: In and Out of Tune

Even though her likeness is in cold stone, I get a warm feeling when I pass the statue of Lucretia Mott. Its place in the U.S. Capitol is especially poignant. Her scheduled lecture in that building was once canceled because she wouldn't promise to be silent about the slavery issue then rocking the nation. It was not until after I decided to read and to write about Lucretia that I learned this is the 200th anniversary of her birth. She was born Lucretia Coffin on Nantucket Island in 1793.

The early nineteenth century was a time of reform, and Lucretia Mott played an important role in many of the movements begun during that period: the abolition of slavery, women's rights, peace, and education. She is one of the founders of Swarthmore College in Pennsylvania. Lucretia became the leading spokesperson for social justice, invited to speak (often as the only woman) on the same platform with William Lloyd Garrison, Theodore Parker, and Ralph Waldo Emerson. Often sharing the same platform were fugitive slaves, some still in their plantation rags.

I had forgotten that it was out of the abolition ferment that the women's right movement was born. Lucretia organized the Anti-Slavery Convention for American Women in 1837. The whole anti-slavery movement split over the issue of admitting women as delegates. So bitter was the feeling over allowing women any place in public life that the women of the Female Anti-Slavery Society were often surrounded by howling mobs, not infrequently struck by the flying glass from smashed windows, or obliged to hold their ground as vitriol, a mixture of caustic chemicals, was thrown at them. On one occasion rioters tried to break up the convention where Lucretia was speaking and actually burned down the hall.

One wonders: what motivated and sustained such persistence against these formidable odds? We find a partial answer in a revolutionary doctrine then being preached by the Quakers. One writer described it as "the unmediated, direct relationship between God and conscience . . . a God of love and social justice. When God told your conscience to fight slavery or to battle for women's equality, you damned well did it."[1]

In Lucretia's remarkable life we find that definition and rendition of conscience. She spoke courageously against blind adherence to dogmas and creeds. Religion, she felt, was not to be found in creeds and forms but "in clean living, in doing right, in common honesty." Her sermons stressed "practical rightness," rather than issues of theology. "Reach the truth; let it go forth," she said. "If these pure principles have their place in us and are brought forth by faithfulness, by obedience, into practice, the difficulties and doubts that we may have to surmount will be easily conquered."[2]

A story demonstrates that "practical rightness" and the surmounting of difficulties and doubts. One cold rainy day Lucretia Mott was on a horse drawn street car. Inside the unheated car, the passengers' feet were gratefully burying themselves in the straw bedded down on the floor. A black woman, looking wretchedly ill, boarded and was sent by the conductor to stand outside on the streetcar's front platform in the cold. When Lucretia pled on the woman's behalf, the conductor noted that it was the law that colored people stand outside. Lucretia went out onto the platform and stood in the cold rain beside the woman. Because she was by then elderly and frail, the other passengers were upset. They begged the conductor to insist that she come in. Lucretia replied, "I cannot go in without this woman." The conductor finally relented.[3]

While Lucretia's prose was eloquent, her singing voice apparently was not. On hearing her sing, Lucretia's mother, Anna, remarked, "Oh, Lucretia, if thee was as far out of town as thee is out of tune, thee wouldn't get home tonight."[4]

Yes, Lucretia Mott was out of tune with the rest of society, but very keenly in tune with her conscience in a beautiful harmony of faith and practice. It is well to ponder her words and example. Looking at how in and out of tune she was, we find a measure for our own lives.

---

1. Source unknown.

2. Anna Davis Hallowell, *James and Lucretia Mott: Life and Letters* (Boston: Houghton, Mifflin and Co., 1884), p. 555.

3. Ibid. pp. 407-408.

4. Lloyd C. M. Hare, *The Greatest American Woman—Lucretia Mott* (New York: American Historical Society Inc., 1884), p. 167.

The Victory Tax and What It Bought

FALL **1993**

This year is the fiftieth anniversary of the 1943 "Victory Tax." This pay-as-you-earn tax on employees' salaries made the employer a tax collector and was enacted to meet the costs of World War II. Let's review the historic connection between war and taxes.

Only ten percent of the War of 1812 was funded by taxpayers. The rest came from borrowing and from the sale of public lands. When the war was over, so were the taxes.

The Civil War revived the Internal Revenue Service, as President Abraham Lincoln imposed the first tax on personal income. Military expenditures mounted to ninety-five percent of the federal budget. If you earned $800 or more, you paid three percent in taxes. Eight years after the war ended, so did the taxes.

World War I military expenditures soared to $35 billion. In 1913, the Sixteenth Amendment to the Constitution was deemed necessary to allow the government to impose income taxes directly on a reluctant population. World War I punched a significant hole in the psychological and institutional barriers between war and peace. At the suggestion of the Bureau of Internal Revenue, thousands of clergymen preached on taxes in their sermons. Only the relative brevity of U.S. involvement in the "war to end all wars" deflected the rush toward more and more centralized government powers. Even so, when the war was over, so were the taxes.

World War II and its 1943 "Victory Tax" struck at the heart of tradition in the United States, as influence and power were thrust upon the military. The war was an organizational and psychological watershed for the military and the nation. A massive effort was initiated by civilian officials to organize and rally society around military-type principals. Education and cajoling were needed to herd millions of citizens into the pool of taxpayers for the first time. Aiding in this effort were the print media, pastors in their pulpits, and the arts. The government hired Irving Berlin to compose a song "You see those bombers in the sky? Rockefeller helped build them; so did I. I paid my income tax today." Even the quackings of Donald Duck helped citizens come to terms with the new taxes. Between 1939 and 1945, the number of taxpayers grew from 4 million to 43 million. This time when the war was over, taxes were not.

Now the Cold War is over and still new patterns are developing. After other wars, the U.S. packed its bags, went home, and closed military production facilities. Sometime during the Cold War, however, the nation forgot, mentally and emotionally, how to re-tool for peace. In the fiftieth year of the Victory Tax, military research and development spending takes sixty percent of all the nation's research funds. All other causes together—health, energy, science, transportation, space, agriculture, education, poverty programs, the environment, etc.—rate a mere forty percent.

We have become the world's largest arms merchant. Profits and jobs drive our sale of conventional arms. Nine million people now make their living on the military payroll. The vigor of an economy fueled by war industries has been a defining experience for an entire generation. This reality has breached the historic divide between civilian and military life and values.

As the Center for Defense Information ruefully observes, military metaphors pervade our language. More and more, our government has adopted fundamental aspects of military culture: its language, forms of organizational structure, decision-making processes, modes of thought, and regimentation. These are employed to approach and address a growing list of non-military problems and situations.

Let us assume that all planned post-Cold War cuts in nuclear weapons will be implemented. If so, in ten years, or by the year 2003, we will still have 8,500 nuclear warheads, or the equivalent of 96,000 Hiroshimas. Why? There are only 3,000 cities that size. We can take comfort that at least we'll build no new nuclear weapons, right? Wrong. The Pentagon will spend $350 billion over the next ten years in research and development of new nuclear weapons as it continues to plan for nuclear war.

We acknowledge the inevitability of death and taxes. It is the connection between the two which grieves and activates the conscience.

The Nature of One's Belief

W hat is the nature of your belief about participation in war? How did you come to hold that belief? How does that belief affect your life? You will have to answer these three questions in writing to be eligible to use the Peace Tax Fund when the Peace Tax Fund Bill becomes law.

Defining that belief and its effect on our lives is precisely the best way to convince Congress to pass the Peace Tax Fund Bill. As we name that belief, sometimes we find government representatives who feel as we do, or who at least offer a degree of understanding, but not always. Here is a quick brush aside I got the other day: "Sorry, we just can't go around accommodating everyone's religious beliefs." Wait a minute! How did freedom of religion come to be so narrowly defined? Wasn't religion so important that its free exercise occasioned the Constitution's First Amendment?

The answer is addressed in a book by Stephen L. Carter, a Yale University professor of constitutional law: *The Culture of Disbelief: How American Law and Politics Trivialize Religious Devotion* (Basic Books, 1993). This book is all the more interesting because President Clinton has read it and now so are others on the White House staff.

The prevailing national attitude seems to be: "Your religion is merely another hobby—like building model airplanes. Keep it under wraps and out of public policy." The courts also tend to hold that an infringement on religious belief is outweighed by the interests of the dominant culture. "If the government decides to destroy your sacred Indian lands, just make some other lands sacred! If you must go to work on your sabbath, it's no big deal! It's just a day off! Pick a different day!" To insist that the state's moral judgments should guide the practices of all religions is to trivialize the idea that faith matters to people.

Carter asserts that in our nation's sensible zeal to keep religion from dominating politics, we have created a political and legal culture that presses the religiously faithful to be other than themselves, *to act as though their faith does not matter to them.* "The consistent message of modern American society is that whenever the demands of one's religion conflict with what one has to do to get ahead, one is expected to ignore the religion's demands and act . . . well . . . *rationally.*"

Religion is not regarded with hostility. But is it progress to have religion regarded as a mere fad, rather than as the very bedrock upon which the faithful build their lives?

The country is troubled when citizens who are moved by their religious understanding are not content either to remain silent or to limit themselves to acceptable platitudes. Why? What is so threatening? There is a higher moral power than the state, we insist. Does that assertion cause the suspicion? Renowned legal scholar Mark Tushnet, who testified at the Peace Tax Fund hearing, says, "It is precisely this ultimate radical possibility of refusing to accept the will of the state that leads to America's political suspicion toward religious belief."

"There is nothing wrong, and much right when a religion refuses to accommodate itself to the policies that the state prefers," says Carter. "A religion is, at its heart, a way of denying the authority of the rest of the world; it is a way of saying, 'No, I will *not* accede to your will.' Taking an independent path . . . exercising the power of resistance . . . is part of what religions are *for* . . . When not domesticated as sacred canopies for the status quo nor wasted by their own self-contradictory grasps at power, the religious live by resisting."

The idea that a group of people will refuse to bow, either to law or to so-called "reason," is a subversive one. "But," says Carter, "religion, properly understood, is a very subversive force, subversive, at least, in a state committed to the proposition that religious ways of looking at the world do not count. No wonder, then, that our political culture seems to be afraid of it." Belief, by definition, entails principles that will not yield. Refusal to yield results in sacrifice. Anyone who believes deeply is a potential martyr. *That*, simply put, is the nature of belief.

Religious-moral-ethical devotion is real. Its language and fervor need not be granted as the sole province of the religious right. The wall of separation between church and state was always intended to prevent governmental interferences in a religion's decisions about what its own theology requires, not the other way around.

Our task of passing the Peace Tax Fund Bill is set in the context of the trivialization of religious devotion. Our responsibility and opportunity is to define more clearly than ever—by faithful words and faithful actions—the answer to the three questions on the nature of our belief. It is our solemn responsibility and great privilege, a duty we owe to both our nation and ourselves.

Boundaries of Conscience

The conscientious objector issue is being cast in a new way in the current health care debate. Newspaper articles with titles such as "Abortion Foes Threaten to Resist Taxes," report that if the health care reform leads to insurance premiums that cover abortion, some are declaring they will not pay.

Michael Kinsley, co-host of CNN's "Crossfire" and a journalist for the *The New Republic*, whose articles are carried by *The Washington Post*, *Los Angeles Times*, and twenty-three other newspapers, says in a recent column, "Right-to-lifers ask a relevant question. 'Why should we be forced to pay taxes for a procedure we find morally repellent?"[1]

Kinsley continues, "There are those who object to military spending and would argue with the same passion as the right-to-lifers, that forcing them to pay for bombs leaves blood on their hands. Should they be allowed to opt out too?" Kinsley's answer is "No."

"The trouble with this tempting argument," explains Kinsley, "is that the national defense is what economists call a 'public good'. It is a benefit that cannot be supplied to one without being supplied to all. How much of it we buy has got to be a collective decision. That's not true of abortions. Furthermore, abortion is a uniquely divisive and emotional issue in American democracy. A substantial minority of the populace believes deeply that it is morally wrong. By comparison, the number of Americans who have deep moral objection to bombers *per se* (as opposed to those who merely believe that the current level of military spending is unnecessary) is quite small."

We appreciate Mr. Kinsley's suggestion that religious liberty is at stake in the argument made by some anti-abortion proponents. We wonder, however, why it is necessary to dismiss the need for conscientious objectors to the military portion of their taxes to make his point about abortion.

There is, after all, legal precedent for conscientious objection "to participation in war in any form." The Supreme Court has reaffirmed the right of the individual to be exempt from participating in war, if his or her beliefs would be violated by that participation. Also, we are not

Johnny-come-latelies to the conscience issue. We have worked for passage of a Peace Tax Fund Bill since 1972. Before that, there have always been people whose consciences prohibited financial participation in war because, as Kinsley says, it is a "blood on your hands" issue.

Kinsley's article excludes conscientious objectors to war because "national defense is a public good." Someone else, the government, decides all citizens should participate in war through taxes. To be divorced from the act, would one not have to refrain from paying that portion of his or her taxes? For people with conscientious scruples the issue is not how much we choose to buy, but whether we can, in conscience, buy it at all. Also, since when is the number of people affected a legitimate reason for dismissing an infringement on religious liberty? That difference in numbers is no more pertinent than enormous difference in numbers between the amount of taxes allocated to abortion versus taxes allocated to the military.

On Capitol Hill, until now, I have observed that most who argued for conscientious objection to abortion drew a boundary excluding conscientious objection to taxes for military force. Fewer and fewer can now make that exclusion. Both issues, many say, are uniquely life-and-death matters and are therefore worthy of special treatment in the tax code.

Recently, one member of Congress became a co-sponsor of the Peace Tax Fund Bill precisely because of the inconsistency of his previous position, which provided conscientious objector status for abortion but not to participating in the military.

Consider the delegation joining together to visit several senators in the hope of following the legislative route taken to pass the Religious Freedom Restoration Act. This delegation includes head congressional liaisons from the National Association of Evangelicals, the General Conference of the Seventh Day Adventists, the Christian Legal Society's Center for Law & Religious Freedom, and the Baptist Joint Committee on Public Affairs. These persons joined members of the Peace Tax Fund's Legislative Advisory Group (who represent the Friends Committee on National Legislation, the Church of the Brethren, Mennonites, the Presbyterian Church, and the Unitarian Universalist Association). This indicates we now have assistance from organizations which, even if they had thought the Peace Tax Fund Bill worthy, did not previously have time to work on it. These organizations are taking a second look at the Peace Tax Fund Bill and are offering their help in making a strong religious freedom argument.

In no way does this mean the two causes will merge. Each will retain its own identity and legislative route. People seem to be learning that, when championing religious freedom, they are on shaky ground when they seek to limit the scope of another's conscience in what can be considered life-and-death issues.

---

1. Michael Kinsley, "TRB From Washington: Bad Choice," *The New Republic*, 13 June, 1994.

A Haven for the Cause of Conscience

Congress shall make no law respecting the establishment of religion, or prohibiting the free exercise thereof.
      –the U.S. Constitution

During Emperor Constantine's reign in the fourth century, the church emerged as a power alongside the state. Bishops were happy to accept Constantine's patronage and in return followed his directives. Empire and church eventually became fused. This union of church and state led to holy wars and inquisitions so abhorrent we still refer to those times as the Dark Ages.

A profound belief in the free exercise of religion motivated the eighteenth-century founders of the United States who named it the first freedom in the founding documents. Many immigrants had experienced the bite of persecution that inevitably results when government either promotes or hinders religion. In naming and elevating this first freedom, the founders underscored the government role with two restrictions: it can neither *establish* religion nor *prohibit* the free exercise of religion. In matters of religion, the government cannot promote or impede, aid or oppose, help or hinder. Together these two clauses guarantee religious freedom for citizens of every faith as well as those who profess no faith at all. The connecting link between the two clauses is freedom of conscience.

Surely, religious liberty is not a subject that should be driving us apart. Yet it is. Disturbingly, the first freedom has currently become a contentious political issue. In fact, the First Amendment is cited repeatedly as an obstacle to private expression of religion.

As one example, a misrepresentation is made of the issue of prayer in public schools. On "Meet the Press," Newt Gingrich recently said, "Most people don't realize it's illegal to pray in public schools." Except by misinformed school administrators, in fact, prayer has not been banned in public schools, nor should it be. Students are free to pray privately, and to have prayer meetings and Bible studies as long as they are not disruptive. Students have a right to share their faith with their friends, wear religious garb and express religious opinions in class and homework. The only prayer that is prohibited by the courts is the prayer that requires government endorsement or approval.

Government support for religion does not enhance religious liberty. Instead, it proves a hindrance. Religions have flourished in this country with unparalleled strength and diversity. Religion prospers most when it is most free. In fact, attempts to have the state advance religion are, in the last analysis, a confession of the religion's weakness. Church and state are not enemies of each other. They simply operate with different authorities. We at the NCPTF office are asking you to argue the religious freedom aspect in your lobbying and letter writing. Our mission in this regard is three-fold.

First, we assert that without a Peace Tax Fund Bill the First Amendment's second clause is being violated. Hear again this testimony from our 1992 hearing:

> [The Peace Tax Fund Bill] seeks to reduce the "inhibiting effect" of current law on the practice of religion.
> *—Michael McConnell, religious freedom expert, University of Chicago Law School*

> If not allowed to follow one's conscience, there can be no religious freedom.
> *—Bishop Thomas J. Gumbleton*

> Faced with the conflict between religious duty and civil law, each of our traditions has tried to no avail to honor the conscience of employees who do not want their tax money used for military purposes. We appeal to an end to what we consider to be the oppressive entanglement of the government in the practice of our faith.
> *—statement by Quaker, Church of the Brethren, and Mennonite denominations*

Second, we ask Congress to serve as a check and balance to another branch of government, the courts. When the Supreme Court refused in *Employment Division v. Smith* (1990) to recognize religious practice as a constitutional right, Congress enacted the Religious Freedom Restoration Act (RFRA) and provided a statutory right. RFRA is hailed as the most significant legislation affecting religious liberty since the Bill of Rights was ratified in 1791. Before RFRA, almost all religious liberty cases were resolved in favor of the government and against the religious claimant. In the three years since RFRA, the process has been reversed. As the courts consistently fail to establish the conscientious right to re-direct military taxes as a constitutional right, we rightly insist that Congress must establish a statutory right, as it did in RFRA.

Third, by our efforts we can safeguard what Roger Williams called "a haven for the cause of conscience." Williams felt conscience is best protected by maintaining a healthy distance between church and government. We would certainly have to agree: a look back reveals that history is strewn with the wreckage of churches and states, each destroyed by unhealthy unions between the two. In these unions each party denies freedom of conscience.

Remember, unlikely allies win religious freedom battles. Some members of Congress have changed their perspectives on the Peace Tax Fund legislation when they have understood that this bill represents an appeal for the freedom to practice one's religion and one's deepest moral-ethical convictions faithfully in all aspects of life.

Conscience: Use It or Lose It

You would have a right to be upset with me if I failed to share with you the spell-binding and enriching experience of the book *Walls: Resisting the Third Reich—One Woman's Story* (Beacon Press, 1974). For twelve terrible years of war and oppression, author Hiltgurt Zassenhaus endured unbelievable hardship and danger. She voluntarily attracted additional adversity to defy external powers from forcing her to cooperate in an evil she could not abide.

Given the job by the Nazi government of censoring the correspondence of Scandinavian political prisoners in Germany, she used the position to smuggle them food, medicine, and a little human kindness. A succession of harrowing close calls resulted. At war's end, she was nominated for the Nobel Peace Prize for saving the Scandinavian prisoners from the firing squads that emptied those prisons with such awful efficiency.

The pressure to comply and survive was intense. "We are to obey orders, not ask questions," she was instructed. "You're young. You can bend. Go along and the future will be yours!"

When I realized to my amazement that Dr. Zassenhaus, now a retired physician in her seventies, lives in the U.S. not an hour from my home, I reached for my telephone. I explained the nature of our work at the NCPTF. "Good for that," she exclaimed. "I am on your side. Can you please come and visit me?"

I inquired about her observations since the Nazi years. She had an instant reply: "I used to get very angry when people suggested that Nazism could also happen here. It was my great error. It can appear whenever there is a climate of apathy, indolence, and fear. It happens every day in my daily life. The same apathy that benumbed the vast majority of good German people, who neither adored nor resisted Nazism, can engulf us. Those marching with guns and boots were relatively small compared with the vast indifferent majority who pretended not to hear or see. The majority of Germans, sooner or later, succumbed to pressure and joined the Party, not because of their convictions, but because they had none."

To make another point, Dr. Zassenhaus related a recent experience when she asked a class of kindergarten children to define conscience. "It tells you when you're bad and when someone hurts," they agreed. "Where is it?" she asked. "Is it on the wall? In the corner? Let's look for it."

"It's not in the corner!" piped one as they searched the room. "It's in me."

"Where inside?" she asked.

"It's in your head," said one. "When I do something bad, my head hurts."

"It's in your stomach," said another. "My stomach gets sore."

"No," said a third. "It's in your skin. Mine gets cold and prickly."

Not long after her day with the kindergarteners, Dr. Zassenhaus, busy with patients, reluctantly accepted a phone call only because of the caller's insistence that his concern was extremely urgent. "This is Danny from the other day," a small voice said. "I've got a conscience problem. My friend is in the hospital. My mother thinks I should visit him, but I want to go to the movies and my friends want me to go to the movies with them."

"What is your conscience telling you?" Dr. Zassenhaus asked. "What would make you feel better tomorrow?" Silence, then: "I'll visit my friend in the hospital. I can go to the movies tomorrow."

"Children know the truth more than older people," Dr. Zassenhaus told me. "Conscience is born with you the same as your two eyes and two arms. If you never used your arms you'd be crippled. It's the same with the conscience. If you don't use it—little by little—it will be insufficient . . . not working any more."

"How could it happen in Germany that people didn't feel the conscience?" she agonized, and then answered her own question. "If you don't use the truth, it dies. That is how concentration camps can happen. People ignored their consciences until they didn't have them anymore. It's a very frightening thing."

The poignant insights of Dr. Zassenhaus seem an especially timely gift as we embark on the busy tasks of 1996: seeking a hearing on the Peace Tax Fund Bill in the Senate; taking advantage of the last year for our lead congressional sponsors; making arguments so strong they have the stature of religious liberty. A prerequisite for this busyness, I now know, is to identify the location of our conscience and to do some painstaking internal work—a task we often avoid, I'm convinced, because it's easier to blame Nazis.

As Dr. Zassenhaus says, talking about conscience is one thing. Listening to it is another.

It's a Belief, Not an Opinion

Two persons, gazing in awe at the great cathedral of Riems, France, struggled to express their wonderment. "Why don't they pile rocks together like this the way they used to?" asked one. "Mon Cheri," came the reply, "in those days people had convictions, not surmises."

"It is the policy of Congress," says the Peace Tax Fund Bill, "to allow conscientious objectors to pay their full tax liability without violating their moral, ethical, or religious beliefs." These words indicate an understanding of the nature of belief. Yet we are impeded in our attempt to be heard because of what most members of Congress and their aides still do not understand. They do not know the history of conscientious objection in the U.S. They do not know that during World War I hundreds of conscientious objectors were sent to prison for their beliefs.

During World War I, 345 conscientious objectors received jail sentences with an average term of 16½ years, and 142 were sentenced to life terms. One-third of those sentences were eventually reduced, but it was not until 1933 that President Roosevelt issued a full pardon and the last conscientious objector of World War I was released from prison.

There were also seventeen death sentences. None of these was carried out, but sixteen conscientious objectors died in prison as a result of mistreatment. Next to its traitors, America meted out its most stringent punishment to its "uncooperative" pacifists. If they removed the army uniform, which was required prison wear for conscientious objectors, they were sent to "the hole," each one in a dark cell, restricted for weeks to bread and water, manacled standing to the bars of their cells for nine hours every day. They had to stand on tip-toe to keep their shackled wrists from carrying the weight of their bodies. When they could no longer sustain that pose, their hands, which carried the weight, swelled and broke open. Some contracted pneumonia. With a diet of only bread and water and no medication, they died. Their bodies were sent home for burial in uniform. One who died of pneumonia was my mother's cousin.

I remember well her grief in relating how that family opened the coffin and recoiled. "What have they done to you? If you would not wear this uniform in life, you shall not wear it in death!" they declared.

They buried their son in his own clothes, then moved to Canada. Their son's convictions, after all, were not founded on opinion. Religious freedom in this country, which they had sacrificed so much to attain, had turned out to be an illusion. It remains incomplete.

Members of Congress and their aides do not know that it was not until 1946 that conscientious objectors immigrating to this country could become naturalized citizens. In that 1946 decision, the Supreme Court said, "In the realm of the conscience, there is a higher moral power than the state." The Court seemed, at least temporarily, to understand the difference between belief and opinion.

Some members of Congress are amazed when they learn the IRS is seizing people's bank accounts. Conscientious objectors lose a child's college education, automobiles, and even houses because they cannot in conscience pay to kill. Legislators see that willingness to risk such penalties is based on more than opinion.

Members of Congress are also surprised when they hear of people living below taxable level, impoverishing themselves and their families, in order not to offend conscience. Some consider that a mark of sincerity.

Unless they are helped to do so, members of Congress and their aides do not take time to consider that citizens could and do provide other services. Mennonites are a small denomination, yet they keep over nine hundred persons working in Third World villages around the world. These workers do not wait to be drafted. They volunteer three to five years of their lives for demanding work at subsistence wages, often in situations of great danger. They have training to improve village life in the areas of health, education and agriculture.

Members of Congress and their aides do not consider this: There is more than one way to defend one's country. Without compelling persuasion, some on Capitol Hill consider something a religious freedom only if they happen to agree with you. Yet the whole point of moral, ethical, and religious freedom is to protect beliefs with which the majority does not agree.

The above stories, and examples of your own, will help Congress to understand the difference between a belief and an opinion. Building cathedrals is slow, patient work. We carefully lay each stone, one at a time.

The Costs of Learning to Kill

The vast majority of soldiers in war do not try to kill the enemy. Throughout history, the majority of men on the battlefield would not attempt to kill the enemy even to save their own lives or the lives of their friends. It is a simple and demonstrable fact that most people have an intense resistance to killing their fellow humans. The compulsion not to kill is stronger than drill, stronger than peer pressure, even stronger than the instinct of self-preservation. This is the contention of Lt. Col. David Grossman, a college ROTC instructor, Army psychologist, and former instructor at West Point.

In his book *On Killing: The Psychological Cost of Learning to Kill in War and Society* (Little, Brown and Co., 1995), Grossman presents these important hypotheses: 1) humans possess a reluctance to kill their own kind; 2) this reluctance can be systematically broken down by standard conditioning techniques; 3) as killing ratio increases, so does post traumatic stress disorder; and 4) the media replicates the army's conditioning techniques and contributes to our society's rising rates of murder and violence.

In World War II, according to Grossman, only fifteen to twenty percent of combat infantry were willing to fire their guns. Those who would not fire did not run or hide. In many cases they were willing to risk great danger to rescue comrades, get ammunition, or run messages, but they simply would not fire at the enemy.

"A firing rate of 15-20% among soldiers," says Grossman, "is like having a literacy rate of 15-20% among proofreaders." Therefore, modern armies have learned to overcome the reluctance to kill. In Korea, about fifty percent of combat infantry were willing to shoot, and in Vietnam the figure rose to over ninety percent. Conditioning techniques, especially the use of human-shaped pop-up cutouts in live fire exercises, overcame soldiers' inhibitions against killing. Grossman points to the desensitization techniques used by the military—the brutality and disorientation of basic training, the use of punishment and reward for previously unfamiliar behavior—as a classic example of psychological conditioning.

Among the things needed for successful conditioning are: constant praise and assurance to the soldier from peers and superiors that he "did the right thing"; parades and monuments; and an unconditionally admiring welcome by friends and society, with the proud display of medals. There is constant danger that combatants will get to know and acknowledge one another as individuals and subsequently may refuse to kill each other. Therefore distances are important: emotional distance ("They were less than animals"), cultural distance (names like "Gook" deny the enemy's humanity), mechanical distance ("I see figures, not people, through night vision glasses"), and moral distance ("If my cause is holy, how can I sin?"). In Vietnam, the process was assisted by a body count. The result of a more efficient killing rate, however, is a vast increase in cases of post traumatic stress disorder. The Vietnam War produced more psychiatric casualties than any other war in American history.

There is also a terrible domestic cost of training reluctant soldiers to kill. High-body-count movies, television violence, and interactive point-and-shoot video games are dangerously similar to military training programs that dehumanize the enemy, desensitize soldiers to the psychological ramifications of killing, and make pulling the trigger an automatic response. They are conditioning our children to kill. A culture raised on Rambo and James Bond is led to believe that combat and killing can be done with impunity, that the soldiers will cleanly and remorselessly wipe "the enemy" from the face of the earth.

"If we had a clear-cut objective of raising a generation of assassins and killers who are unrestrained by either authority or the nature of the victim, it is difficult to imagine how we could do a better job," Grossman says. "We are reaching that stage of desensitization at which the infliction of pain and suffering has become a source of entertainment: vicarious pleasure rather than revulsion. We are learning to kill, and we are learning to like it."

Our prophets have been right. If we threaten to kill and make good on that threat through military production and training, our violence will surely turn back on us. The startling examples of de facto conscientious objection in this book are far from unique. We are all conscientious objectors at heart, and the costs of "learning war" ravage all sides.

The Peace Tax Fund Bill at Twenty-Five

D o you remember "the way we were" twenty-five years ago when the Peace Tax Fund Bill was first introduced in Congress? Perhaps you were reading *Jonathan Livingston Seagull* or *The Best and the Brightest* or perusing the first issue of *MS* magazine.

In 1972 President Nixon made historic trips to China and the Soviet Union. He and Vice President Agnew were re-elected in the biggest Republican landslide in history. That same year police arrested five men in a burglary of Democratic Party headquarters, a harbinger of the president's downfall. The Democratic Party proved unable to support its candidate, Senator George McGovern, who vowed to end U.S. military presence in Vietnam. McGovern also supported cuts in defense spending and amnesty for those who had chosen prison or exile over military service. Alabama governor George Wallace was shot while campaigning in the presidential primary and was paralyzed from the waist down.

The mining of Haiphong Harbor and other ports was ordered by Nixon. The North Vietnamese move into South Vietnam resulted in heavy air bombardment of the North. Body counts were used as a measure of U.S. progress. The Paris peace talks stalled for months after the U.S. walked out; then resumed; then again reached an impasse. Two strategic arms (SALT) agreements between the U.S. and USSR. limited each country to two antiballistic missile systems of 100 missiles each.

The trial of peace activists, the Harrisburg Seven, ended with a hung jury after federal prosecutors moved to drop all conspiracy charges against Philip Berrigan and six others. (They had been accused of plotting to kidnap Henry Kissinger and blow up underground heating tunnels in Washington, D.C.) Terrorists entered the Olympic village in Munich, Germany. In the end, eleven Israeli coaches and athletes plus a number of the terrorists were dead. The Supreme Court ruled state death penalties unconstitutional as cruel and unusual punishment.

Making a difference

Yes, it is twenty-five years, and counting. So, should we throw a party or wear mourning clothes to grieve twenty-five more years of rights denied? Now is an appropriate time to ponder this question and assess where we are as a movement.

"What about shelf life?" a senator was asked. "Is the fact that the Peace Tax Fund Bill has been pending for years a liability?" His firm answer was, "No. Some of the most important legislation in history took twenty years or more. Good ideas do eventually win." Indeed. Anti-tobacco groups worked many years before things suddenly began to break. The bill to allow women the right to vote was introduced in forty-one different sessions of Congress before it was finally passed in 1920. Slavery is an example of a long-haul struggle to grant what we now take for granted. I look forward to the day when we will be incredulous at the thought of a time when granting status for conscientious objection to military taxes was controversial.

Notable among the changes in past years is a shift in public perception. Dismissed too easily in the beginning as misguided anti-Vietnam War radicals, we are now seen as a respected organization whose just claim for freedom of conscience has been denied. The 1992 hearing on the Peace Tax Fund Bill was a major milestone. It provided a wealth of positive comment and interpretation, helped clarify the legal issues involved, showed the depth of conviction of the bill's supporters, and enhanced our profile in Congress.

Ecumenical support has grown far beyond the historic peace churches to include mainline bodies, and, more recently, groups such as the National Association of Evangelicals and the Christian Legal Society. As demonstrated by last November's meeting with a White House official, I can now call up a broad delegation of persons for important visits with Congress or the Administration. This spectrum of pacifist and non-pacifist, political left and right, demonstrates the depth of conviction of the Peace Tax Fund Bill's supporters far better than words. In fact, that is what got us into the White House and what prompted an invitation to return.

The international spin-offs are also notable. Since 1986 we have participated in international conferences in Germany, The Netherlands, Italy, Spain, Belgium, and England. A new organization, Conscience and Peace Tax International, was formed by this body. It has already been granted lobbying status in some European parliaments and is seeking that status in the United Nations. This international exchange has been a rich learning experience for us. Our contribution is also appreciated. The first German peace tax fund legislation was a direct translation from the

U.S. bill. Our materials have been translated into a number of languages and are used to persuade members of other parliaments. The voice of conscientious objection to military taxes is heard literally around the world.

Changing with the times

The Peace Tax Fund Bill was born amid a war opposed by more than half the population. There was immense despair but enough hope to propel an energetic peace movement. Now peace is an issue which is almost invisible. Openings for members on the once powerful Foreign Affairs committees go begging. Twenty-five years ago, Congress was composed largely of the liberal side of the Democratic Party. The momentum now is controlled by the conservative side of the Republican Party.

In the same twenty-five years other groups have flourished and succumbed. I believe we have endured because we have adjusted. We couched our arguments to touch others' sense of morality in the context of the times. Our initial peace argument has been augmented with cogent arguments based on the First Amendment. Conscience against killing fellow humans does not change with the times, though expressions of conscience may. Our message is all the more clear, we are told, because we have persisted over the long term. Expressions of our deepest convictions will get attention, no matter what the times.

Does the Term *Religious Freedom* Exclude Some Conscientious Objectors?

WINTER **1998**

The percentage of conscientious objectors (COs) who claim religion as their primary motive has declined. Religious objectors now make up only a minority of the total number of conscientious objectors—between fourteen and eighteen percent—in European countries. The U.S. does not keep track, but during the Vietnam War an increasing number of draftees stated moral, ethical, or humane—rather than religious—objections.

According to studies, this pattern of acceptance of non-religious COs goes through familiar stages: 1) official recognition of conscientious objection is granted but is usually limited to traditional peace sects such Mennonites, Quakers, and Church of the Brethren; 2) authorities recognize a broader religious criterion for conscientious objection and allow some forms of alternative civilian service; and 3) secular motives are accepted along with (in some countries) selective objection to particular wars and/or nuclear weapons.

If most COs are not religious, why did we add the name "Religious Freedom" to the Peace Tax Fund Bill? Are we excluding sincere COs?

No. The term *religious*, as used in this case, is a legal term and excludes no one. It protects equally the freedom of religion and the freedom *not* to have a religion. The United Nations Charter of Human Rights enshrined in 1993 the "right to freedom of thought, conscience and religion." Thus, the Peace Tax Fund Bill uses the term *religious freedom* in its broadest sense of referring to religion, conscience, and moral beliefs.

Religion, however, is still used as a base-line measurement. When the Supreme Court greatly liberalized the rights of COs in the 1970s, it extended the definition to include "a meaningful belief occupying in the life of its possessor a place parallel to that filled by the God of those admittedly qualified for the exemption." Secular criteria for conscientious objection followed closely after recognition of religiously stated motives, not before. Opinion surveys show greater acceptance of religiously motivated COs. While membership in an organized religion is still considered a mark of sincerity, legal systems now make accommodation for the reasoned and articulate secular CO.

Clearly, many groups who are joining us now say that peace is not the door through which they entered to lend enthusiastic support, but rather the First Amendment protection of freedom of conscience/religion. As a result, active support for the Religious Freedom Peace Tax Fund (RFPTF) Bill has grown beyond what many of us would have predicted. Two visits to the White House and a re-write of the RFPTF Bill prompted the White House to request that Treasury officials meet with us.

In a face-to-face dialogue at the Treasury Department, we learned first-hand about IRS questions and perceptions. Our delegation indicated a desire to work cooperatively to find a way for conscience against war taxes to be accommodated in law. The delegation was supported by phone calls made by the Religious Action Center for Reformed Judaism and the Legal Counsel for the National Council of Churches. Support at this level would have been hard to imagine a few years ago. In the meeting, the Treasury officials promised to consider the RFPTF proposal among themselves.

As you work locally, you will be able to approach our new allies in forming delegations to meet with your own Washington representatives. Fresh opportunities for dialogue emerge for us at all levels: local, national and international. The spectrum of pacifist and non-pacifist, political left and right, demonstrates the breadth and depth of support and calls for serious consideration.

If we are careful to use the inclusive "freedom of religion and/or conscience" language, we find we can work with a broader scope of organizations than we had thought. The term "religious freedom" is not exclusive, and it still carries a powerful message.

Loving the Hell out of People

Walking With the Wind by U.S. Representative John Lewis (Simon and Schuster, 1998) is a riveting book, a must read. It recounts the author's part in the nonviolent civil rights struggle that rocked this nation and forced it to face its conscience. The son of poor Alabama sharecroppers, who as a child preached to the chickens, Lewis now dines with heads of state and is a member of the U.S. Congress.

You will be awed and grateful that Lewis, the main sponsor of the Religious Freedom Peace Tax Fund Bill in the U.S. House of Representatives, is this manner of person. From the freedom rides of 1961, during which Lewis was repeatedly brutalized and imprisoned, to the civil rights march on "Bloody Sunday" in Selma, Alabama, where he suffered a fractured skull during an attack by state troopers, he maintained a quiet dignity with intellect, faith, courage and perseverance. I warn you, this story will force you to take a measure of yourself, and in my case at least, to realize there is still much growing up to do.

Here are some of the book's lessons:

1. "Keep your eyes on the prize," which John Lewis describes as a "more perfect union" and "a beloved community."

2. It is essential to endure pain and suffering. The tears, and the lives lost, make a redemptive difference in society.

3. Suffering is not enough. As Lewis says, "It can be nothing more than a sad and sorry thing without the presence on the part of the sufferer of a graceful heart, a heart that holds no malice toward the inflictors of his or her suffering."

4. Training is important, as indicated in the words of nonviolence instructor James Lawson. Lawson had filed for conscientious objector status during the Korean War rather than register for the draft, and he spent fourteen months in jail for his refusal to serve.

In training sessions, Lawson was tough. "When you can truly understand and *feel,* even as a person is cursing you to your face, even as he is spitting on you, or pushing a lit cigarette into your neck, or beating you with a truncheon—if you can understand and feel even in the midst of those critical and often physically painful moments that your attacker is as much a victim as you are, that he is a victim of the forces that have shaped and fed his anger and fury, then you are well on your way to the nonviolent life" (77).

"It was not enough, [Lawson] would say, simply to endure a beating. It was not enough to resist the urge to strike back at an assailant. 'That urge can't *be* there,' he would tell us . . . 'You have to have no *desire* to hit back. You have to *love* that person who's hitting you. You're *going* to love him'" (85).

Love is a way of life

This love is not simply a technique or strategy to be pulled out when needed. This is a way of life that permeates each moment from the monumental to the mundane. "This sense of love, this sense of peace, the capacity for compassion, is something you carry inside yourself every waking minute of the day. It shapes your response to a curt cashier or a driver cutting you off in traffic" (77). Ouch.

This is a more all-encompassing love than loving something that's lovely to you. Says Lewis, this is "a love that accepts and embraces the hateful and the hurtful. It is a love that recognizes the spark of the divine in each of us, even in those who would raise their hand against us, those we might call our enemy. This love realizes that emotions of the moment and constantly shifting circumstances can cloud that divine spark. Pain, ugliness and fear can cover it over, turning a person toward anger and hate. It is the ability to see through those layers of ugliness, to see further into a person than perhaps that person can see into himself, that is essential to the practice of nonviolence" (77).

"Love the hell out of them," Lewis remembers Martin Luther King, Jr., saying, "and he meant that literally. If there is hell in someone, if there is meanness and anger and hatred in him, we've got to *love* it out" (78).

The Arms Race with Ourselves

As we look toward hosting the eighth International Conference on War Tax Resistance and Peace Tax Campaigns, I recall the first such gathering in West Germany in 1986. Attendees at that conference were shocked by the huge proportion (around fifty percent) of U.S. annual federal spending directed toward the military. We in turn were envious of percentages as low as five or ten percent in Europe.

There is some good news. World military spending is down from $1.2 trillion in 1985 to $785 billion in 1998, according to the London-based International Strategic Studies Program. And yes, there is bad news. In the same period the U.S. share jumped from thirty percent to thirty-six percent of that total. Yet the U.S. military is starving, according to bestselling author William Greider in *Fortress America: The American Military and the Consequences of Peace* (PublicAffairs, 1999). Our military, he says, has come to resemble a starving body. It must keep feeding, he says, only now it is feeding on itself.

"The U.S. military-industrial complex, as we have known it, is in the process of devouring itself, literally and tangibly," because of over-spending on weapons systems, asserts Greider. What cannot endure long, he says, is the "awesome interlocking structure of armed forces, industrial interests, and political alliances that has sprawled across American public life and purpose for two generations" (ix). Admiral Eugene Carroll of the Center for Defense Information says, "It appears we are in an arms race with ourselves."

Greider says citizens consciously avert their eyes and refuse to see that the emperor has no clothes. I have to admit that as a pacifist I, too, have averted my eyes and have chosen to remain somewhat naive about details of the enormity of the numbers and deadly ability of our armaments. Greider reveals almost inconceivable levels of waste and confusion in the hundreds of billions of dollars squandered by the U.S. military in the post-Cold War world.

Fortress America possesses target overkill in staggering dimensions. Greider cites a 1996 Government Accounting Office study which documents the redundancies: "The services already have at least 10 ways to hit 65 percent of the thousands of expected ground targets in two major regional conflicts" (42).

It is all because of "them" that this juggernaut—the biggest military force in the world—lumbers on. The nation's political and military leaders seem to be searching forlornly for an enemy, a "they," that can restore purpose to the country's mighty armaments.

Here are some examples cited by Greider of your tax dollars at work:

- We have so many tanks that the Army has taken to dumping them in the ocean to form coral reefs—and then asking to buy even more.

- The Air Force has so many long-range bombers it can't even afford to keep them in the air—and still it wants to build more.

- Tax dollars furnish money for research and development of new weapons systems, which are then sold to other countries.

- The power of the arms lobby is pressing for an enlarged NATO, not for security but to establish markets for new weapons.

- Ten years ago there were fifteen arms manufacturers competing for two-thirds of the Pentagon's contracts. Now there are only three, and their bills to the U.S. government continue to swell.

- This nation spends twelve times more on promoting arms sales abroad than on environmental technologies.

Here is another caution. Just as our government is under ever-increasing control and influence by the arms industry, we are becoming increasingly isolated from world opinion and our own people. Greider points out that "the rest of the world is not blind. It can see America planning and producing spectacular new weapons systems when its arsenal is already overwhelmingly superior and deeply redundant. Other nations, large and small, ask themselves: What do those Americans have in mind for their new super-weapons? Is it self-defense or dominion?" (180).

Whether their nation's military spending percentage is five percent or fifty percent, those who will gather at the international conference in July share an outrage and a dream. What if we employed that money instead to take away the provocation of wars?

Eighth International Conference:
Many Ripples Make a Wave

SUMMER **2000**

How I wish you could all have been there! "We assert the right not to pay for war whether that participation is physical of financial." That was the theme of this biennial International Conference on War Tax Resistance and Peace Tax Campaigns. So strong is the bond between us that the campaigns have created their own non-governmental organization to testify at the UN: Conscience and Peace Tax International! Three countries who wanted badly to attend sent written reports only because delegates were denied visas by our government: Bangladesh, Nepal and Guinea. Here are the conference reports:

Bangladesh: Aims of the Bangladesh Interreligious Council for Peace and Justice are to provide a center for training, mediation, conflict resolution and peace studies. It researches and documents these subjects on local, national and international levels.

Belgium: Belgium is a federal state, comprised of three regions: Flanders, Wallonia, and bilingual Brussels. Two campaigns exist, one Flemish and the other French-speaking. One campaign has introduced a peace tax bill and the largest one will send a new bill to members of the Green Party. Seven percent of each person's income tax goes to the military. International law is increasingly cited in war tax resistance (WTR) court cases.

Canada: The peace tax bill is moving, but slowly. The campaign changed the bill to stipulate where the money from conscientious objectors does not go, and deleted the section stipulating where the money must go. The campaign includes a French-speaking group in Quebec. Since 1978, "peace trusters" have put their resisted money in a trust fund to be held until it is requested.

Germany: The courts turn down WTR cases. The campaign changed its tactic from circulating its own bill to asking members of Parliament for their suggestions on how the constitutional right to freedom of conscience can become effective for conscientious objectors to military taxes. Besides lobbying, the campaign seeks public support from religious, political, and peace groups and well-known persons.

Guatemala: "Working on peace puts your body in danger. We are afraid," says Cezar Flores, reminding us of the price many pay for following their consciences. Two hundred thousand have died in Guatemala and two hundred communities have been disappeared. "Weapons do not save lives or build a community."

Honduras: Closely tied with the Guatemalan campaign, Mennonites began working on legislation in Honduras in the 1980s. Central American countries run the Latin American Anabaptist Center, teaching peace and equal justice courses.

Hungary: "It is possible to invent war tax resistance and peace tax campaigns," Janos Ratkai reported. A gentleman in Hungary who knew nothing about such movements in other countries began work in these areas. The nonviolent peace movement is ten years old. The campaign used the legislation from eight other countries to fashion its own. Their bill has received some positive response from members of Parliament. A legislative hearing was held last autumn. (Note: Hungary says our literature should be shared on the web and translated into many languages to encourage fledgling movements.)

India: Gandhi-in-Action formed "Conscience India" in 1997. Requests have been made to Parliament to introduce peace tax legislation. All national political parties have been asked to take up this matter. The prime minister and president of Indian National Congress responded to the communication. Conscience India and Gandhi-in-Action organized mass fasting to oppose Pakistan's nuclear testing. Persons from both countries participated.

Italy: A bill providing conscientious objection to military service was passed in 1998. That bill also mandated a government study on means of nonviolent defense; it is also intended to "study a way of fiscal choice that citizens could pay, not for armed defense, but for objectors' civil service." Another bill mandates meetings between governmental institutions and army objectors. Legal recognition of the right not to pay for the Army will have a difficult time finding approval. Cosimo Tomiselli says that a greater possibility is seen with a bill to allow payment for the bureau to build a Nonviolent Defense.

Japan: The main goal of the campaign is to remind government and the public of Japan's constitution, which forbids an armed force. Courts inform resisters they have no right to make appeals. At the campaign's beginning in 1974 many citizens and organizations, such as labor unions, were interested in tax resistance. They lost interest after learning the money would not be returned to them. Resistance accelerated during the Gulf War.

Netherlands: War tax resistance has declined steadily, cases have been lost in the Supreme Court, and the Green Party no longer supports the bill due to changes in personnel. "Euros for Peace," the new name for the campaign, represents its emphasis. The campaign now lobbies government to spend money on peacebuilding missions. Members send protests to military use of their taxes with their tax forms. The campaign seeks to broaden the article on conscientious objection to include objection to the military destination of tax money.

Nepal: The Organization for Solidarity, Equality, Environment and Development seeks to educate citizens as to the extent of governmental corruption. The government has recently added a value-added tax to help fund a standing army in this impoverished country. Peace organizations organize seminars, talk programs, peace marches, and work camps. A goal is to seek enforcement of the Comprehensive Test Ban Treaty.

Nigeria: Successive governments, even since 1967 and the restoration of democracy, have had more funds budgeted to the Ministry of Defense than to agriculture, education, health, or industrial production. Yet not a single bullet is produced in Nigeria. This issue is being addressed by a coalition of NGOs, which may be persuaded to incorporate peace tax into its proposals for increasing democracy and replacing the current constitution.

Norway: The first ever peace tax fund bill was introduced this June. Frank Sivertsen, who performed alternative service as a conscientious objector, was able to use three months of that time to lobby full-time for the peace tax fund bill! Support for the measure comes from the Christian Democratic Party, the Socialist Party, and many Norwegian notables. Other members of Parliament have indicated they may give support.

Russia: Conscientious objection to military service is recognized in the constitution, but legislation to put this recognition into practice has not yet been passed. Sergei Nikitin heard about the peace tax fund movement four years ago and has since written on the subject. He has worked for the peace tax fund movement through the Friends House Moscow and in his hometown near St. Petersburg.

Spain: After a massive campaign which sent many hundreds to prison, compulsory military service was ended last year! Compulsory military taxes are now the target of the campaign, though there is no legislation yet. Tax resistance has received no judicial response from the exchequer. Tax resisted money ($30,000 U.S.) from about two thousand people funds conscientious objection groups in Turkey, Paraguay, and Colombia as well as humanitarian projects in other countries.

United Kingdom: The campaign is twenty years old. Two staff persons, Jon Nott and Jackie Hoskins, lobby and produce literature to help others to lobby. A parliamentary petition to measure support for the British Peace Tax Fund Bill was signed by forty-six members of Parliament. In October, 2000, the European Convention on Human Rights becomes law in the U.K. Lobbyists will focus on bringing tax law into line with human rights.

European Union: The European Bureau on Conscientious Objection is asking that member states of the EU recognize conscientious objection to military service almost as a requirement for membership. If a positive comment is gained from the Human Rights Commission, this could be used to add credence to European campaigns. The average annual military expenditure for each EU resident is about four hundred fifty Euros (about $450).

There is a familiar ring to various government responses: garnishing wages, attaching bank accounts, and in rare instances, prison. Some campaigns report loss of traction. Peace, they say, is not a hot topic and militaries are promoting a "humanitarian" profile. Courts generally do not honor conscientious objection to military taxes. International law, the right to "freedom of thought, conscience and religion," is increasingly cited in WTR court cases. Each campaign seems like a lonely voice in its national political dialogue. But together we sense a gathering global chorus. The bond between us is powerful. That, and the fact that we have created our own NGO in the United Nations, lends credence and confidence to each campaign.

A War Memorial to Conscientious Objectors

Universal military training had come to West Prussia (now Poland), so in 1880 my grandfather and his young family moved to Russia in search of freedom of conscience. Four years later, after enormous hardships, which, one by one, took the lives of all five of the children, the family moved to the United States to find the elusive freedom. Here, however, my grandfather's nephew was imprisoned because he was a conscientious objector (CO). He died in prison. His body was sent home for burial in the army uniform which he had refused to wear. It is not surprising that among my grandfather's papers I found a booklet with this chilling letter:

> December ———, 1918. Today marks the end of another Conscientious Objector, who underwent solitary confinement here in prison. . . . Four COs . . . were hung up by the wrists so that only their toes touched the cold damp floor, which was thirty feet below the ground. They were deprived of their over clothing and were forced to live in the stench of their own excrement. After four days without food and under these horrible conditions they got scurvy, and were sent here, to this prison. Here they refused to work for the Military, and consequently were put in solitary. . . . Today we heard Captain ——— hurriedly ask for permission for ——— to see his relative before he died. The parents of the first . . . to die had just been here to bury their son about a week before. Two are now dead of the four. . . . They have made the supreme sacrifice for liberty and their deaths must not be in vain.

For COs in World War I, there were 17 death sentences, 142 life terms in prison, and 345 prison sentences where the average term was 16½ years. None of the death sentences was carried out, and one-third (185) of the sentences were eventually reduced, but it was not until 1933 that President Roosevelt issued a full pardon and the last conscientious objector of World War I was released from prison.

Non-religious objectors received the worst treatment. Many of these were sent to "the hole," each one in a dark cell, restricted for weeks to bread and water. They were manacled, standing, to the bars of their cells for nine hours every day. They were struck, placed in solitary confinement, and hung by their thumbs. As I lobby, I find that few know these facts. Some, I suspect, do not believe them.

The number of war memorials in the nation's capital is burgeoning. The Vietnam War wall has the names of 58,200 beloved persons who lost their lives in that war. Now the Korean War has its memorial, which shows statues of soldiers trudging with their weapons.

This Veterans' Day, ground was symbolically broken for yet another World War II memorial in the nation's capital to pay homage to the "generation that waged the most monumental, most unequivocally righteous struggle in history."[1] The statue of the marines raising the flag on Iwo Jima is not considered adequate to memorialize all of those soldiers.

The new memorial, however, is controversial because of its location and size. Many argue it is ill-conceived, out of place, and that it ruptures the serenity of the national mall. The mall is a magnificent untouched space that offers a two-mile-long vista, extending from the Lincoln Memorial to the Washington Monument to the U.S. Capitol. The new World War II memorial is to be erected directly in that line of sight. There is to be a pool with an as yet unknown architectural element in the center, surrounded by seventeen-foot-high granite columns with wreaths. There will be fifty-six of these. Another element will be a stone wall, making it nearly impossible to walk directly east-west across the Mall. Two arches representing the Atlantic and Pacific fronts, rising a massive forty-one feet above the mall, will dwarf anything else around.

A few weeks ago a memorial to Japanese Americans who served in World War II took its place among Washington's monuments. While it purports to honor the patriotism of a selected group of citizens, this memorial also reminds us of our country's shame. Soon after the 1941 attack on Pearl Harbor, the federal government declared that Americans of Japanese ancestry were "enemy agents" and issued an executive order authorizing the internment of Japanese Americans. More than one hundred twenty thousand were imprisoned in concentration camps for no reason other than their ancestry. When the government eventually opened military service to them, 2,686 volunteered.

One writer declared that with the proposed World War II memorial and the one honoring Japanese Americans, all World War II patriots will have been recognized. I beg to differ. The Peace Tax Campaign in London has placed a memorial stone to conscientious objectors of past wars. It stands in a prominent park. So why don't we take the initiative to place a memorial to COs in our nation's capital? Do you think such a proposal is worth the effort?

Read again the last sentence of the 1918 letter recounting the deaths of conscientious objectors: *"They have made the supreme sacrifice for liberty and their deaths must not be in vain."*

1. Charles Krauthammer "The WW II Memorial: Inadequate and out of Place," *The Washington Post*, 28 July 2000, p. A25.

Shalom: It's a Mighty Challenge

Mention the Middle East these days and what response do you get? Shoulders shrug, eyes roll, and expressions of helplessness ensue. Can nonviolence rescue dreams of living in peace? A book we've been sent recently deals with that inquiry.

"How is it possible for a Jewish person to be nonviolent, especially after the Holocaust?" is an often-asked question. *The Challenge of Shalom: The Jewish Tradition of Peace and Justice* (New Society, 1994) shows that "never again" doesn't necessarily mean taking up arms. This refreshing volume, edited by Murray Polner and Naomi Goodman, features prominent contributors on controversial topics. It includes sections on tradition, the Holocaust, Israel, conscientious objection, civil disobedience. The editors and authors have been deeply associated with the Jewish Peace Fellowship, which deals with the unique pressures felt by the Jewish pacifist.

The authors verify that a powerful peace tradition exists in all branches of Judaism: Orthodox, Conservative, Reconstructionist, and Reform. The Jewish tradition of peace is often obscured, the writers contend, or it has been brushed aside as passive and impractical. The imperative for peace and active nonviolence is not only possible but preferable—yes, even given the awful history of pogroms and slaughters.

While never forgetting the mass murders, the editors seek to avoid political manipulation of the sacrifices of the martyred. However, they question seriously whether violence and counter-violence are the best defenses against the possibility of future horrors.

Some of the emphases of the Jewish tradition coincide with some convictions which today constitute pacifism. Consciously or unconsciously, subtle social and religious influences have created receptiveness to modern pacifism. In fact, both conscience and consequences persuade. In the nuclear age, war as an option has been eradicated. "Humane warfare" is an oxymoron. Armed might cannot be used as an instrument of justice.

Many authors contributing to the book are pacifist. Rabbi Albert Axelrad, a long time peace activist, calls himself a "pacifoid" who would make a reluctant exception to his pacifism and choose warfare if Israel's existence were threatened.

Rabbi Henry Schwarzchild, whose family fled Nazi Germany in the 1930s, is quoted: "The men and women of my generation have gone through a world war, the Holocaust, Stalinism and Vietnam—not to speak of other mass bloodlettings. I have seen enough unnatural deaths to last a lifetime. I know that I, like other men and women, have no choice but to die—only once, but some time. I do, however, have a choice as to whether I will die with human blood on my hands."

Rabbi Philip Bentley's chapter interested me because he testified at our Peace Tax Fund hearing before Congress in 1992. Here's some of what he said then:

> Those of us who are conscientious objectors to war are distressed at having to pay for and support wars with our tax dollars. We believe that war-making is morally wrong. The words "just," "moral," and "right" cannot, in our view, ever be used to describe a war. . . . We object also to the use of our tax dollars to promote the manufacture of weapons, which encourages and abets a trade in deadly force to whoever has the money to pay for it. . . . Jewish law says that whoever sells a weapon bears responsibility for its use. We are pained at the thought that we support such sales with our tax payments. . . . The enactment of this bill would be, in my opinion, a great act of decency in allowing for the fuller participation of a religious and spiritual minority in the American polity. . . . Enactment would be both right and wise.[1]

The editors' stated hope is that reconciliation will end the support of some Jews and some Palestinians for violent actions carried out in the name of collective defense. Unsung heroes on both sides work daily at reconciliation—some in quiet ways and some in situations of danger. It's a shame their stories are not highlighted in our press.

It seems the only killing in human history not done in revenge is when Cain killed Abel. All the rest have been revenge killings. It reminds me of an old proverb, "If you're going to seek revenge, you should dig two graves."

---

1. Full text of hearing available in *Congressional Record*, Serial 102-98, pp. 1-295.

Cassandra's Dilemma

Cassandra was the beautiful daughter of the last king of Troy. The god Apollo fell in love with her, but she refused his advances. To win her affections, Apollo made a proposal: if Cassandra agreed to love him, he would give her the gift of prophecy. Cassandra accepted the bargain and was granted the ability to see the future. Now she could warn people of impending catastrophes and save the world!

Still, she could not bring herself to love Apollo, a fact that filled him with rage. Cassandra's gift could not be taken back, but the god took cruel revenge. He begged her for a single kiss. She consented. When their lips touched, Apollo breathed into Cassandra's mouth in such a way that no one would ever believe her prophecies. Thereafter, the doomed Cassandra could see dangers threatening others but could not prevent them. She warned the Trojans that the Greeks would attack. They did nothing because they did not believe her. She warned that enemy soldiers were hidden inside the Trojan horse. Her warnings were unheeded and Troy fell forever.

I've never spurned Apollo as far as I know, yet even without his kiss, I know how Cassandra feels. Surely you too are familiar with Cassandra's dilemma of issuing unpopular warnings of avoidable danger and having them go unheeded.

I owe the ideas in this article to the book *Believing Cassandra: An Optimist Looks at a Pessimist's World* (Chelsea Green, 1999), in which author Alan Atkisson spells out Cassandra's global concerns: "At risk today are thousands of species, billions of people's lives, not to mention humanity's collective innocence." Many would also see a dire warning in the violence of still more increases in military spending when human needs and nature's needs are so great. This can create intolerable problems of pollution, economic distress, and festering conflict over dwindling supplies of income and resources.

Our dilemma is ancient. The Old Testament/Torah informs us that biblical prophets were well-versed in Cassandra's dilemma. The slave-holding Egyptians were warned to let the Israelites go, but they ignored Moses and lost their first-born sons. The inhabitants of Sodom and

Gomorrah orgied on toward destruction, despite warnings. There are many similar stories.

I find Noah's story particularly poignant. "For as in those days before the flood they were eating and drinking, marrying and giving in marriage, until the day Noah entered the ark" (Matthew 24:38). People were going about business as usual. They thought Noah's ark a folly. Why was survival on earth threatened? According to the ancient text, "Now the earth was corrupt in God's sight, and the earth was filled with violence" (Genesis 6:11). Our calling is like Noah's: to shepherd all species (including ours) to a safe ark away from this flood of violence and its repercussions. The planet is our ark and we're on it for keeps.

Why is it so hard to alert the body politic to global trouble? Why are warnings are so notoriously ineffective, and why do people, even those who believe you, still do nothing? One answer is that people simply don't want to know. We are resistant to hearing things that could be devastating. Speaking about the environmental crisis, Al Gore says, "The minds of the people are unprepared to accept the political leadership that these conclusions would compel."

Cassandra's dilemma comes with weighty emotions of fear, anger, and sadness, which can frighten and overpower us. We shake our heads in puzzlement. We cry. We sigh. In sharing these emotions, we discover a surprising new sense of hope and purpose.

Postscript, 9-11-01

We too were "going about business as usual." Rosa Packard and I were minutes outside New York City on our way to represent Conscience and Peace Tax International at a UN conference. As news of what had happened so near us dawned, fear took hold. Rosa's daughter-in-law worked on the forty-seventh floor of the World Trade Center. After several intense hours, we finally learned that she was safe, having escaped death by only a few minutes. My friend's daughter at the Pentagon was also safe. Now we could mourn for the thousands we do not know.

This is a time of deep self-examination for prophets who may have pointed out that human misery breeds support for terrorism. They are not allowed a self-righteous "I told you so!" Remember, however, that "success" for the prophet is measured by repentance, a turning back, a change of behavior that will avoid further steps to catastrophe.

It seems appropriate to end with the words of Phyllis and Orlando Rodriguez whose son, Greg, is missing in the World Trade Center: "Not in our name . . . Our government is heading in the direction of violent revenge, with the prospect of sons, daughters, parents, friends in distant lands dying, and nursing further grievances against us. It is not the way to go. It will not avenge our son's death."

Peace and Security

With shocking suddenness our illusion of safety has vanished. We understand painfully the results of violence which many must bear in addition to desperate want. Our vulnerability humbles us.

For me, equally as shocking as the tumbling towers is the fact that for several weeks, I was barred from Senate and House office buildings, my usual lobbying beat. An answering machine states a senator's inaccessibility. Several of my Capitol Hill friends are taking Cipro because of exposure to letters laced with anthrax. Amid the shocks, there is a sense of déjà vu, especially for those of us who have lived through past wars.

First, pacifists are shamed and blamed. Here are some quotes from recent columns in the *Washington Post*: "The American pacifists . . . are on the side of future mass murders of Americans."[1] "They are objectively pro-terrorist. . . . The pacifist position is evil . . . largely reactionary, largely incoherent . . . opposition to war is rooted in America-hatred, is intellectually dishonest, elitist and hypocritical."[2] Pretty strong stuff.

Second, dissent seems to end where war begins. Opposing voices are muted and marginalized. Journalists who pose skeptical questions have been inundated with furious responses calling them disgraceful, even traitorous. Polls show that a substantial majority support war "even if many thousands of innocent civilians are killed." What happened? I thought tolerance of dissent and respect for a diversity of beliefs were among the nation's most cherished ideals.

Also, in times like this, national self-interest becomes the will of God. Religious people equate God with country. A tribal god smiles on all that its nation does.

Three days after the horrors of September 11, I returned to Capitol Hill to lobby for the Religious Freedom Peace Tax Fund Bill. In one office, the congressman's chief of staff began our visit with a cautionary, "I'm not a pacifist, Marian."

I asked, "Okay, so what kind of a 'not-pacifist' are you? The kind who seeks ten-fold revenge or the 'weeping prophet' who truly seeks an outcome of peace which implies justice?" I mentioned the hundreds of thousands of children who have died in Iraq since the Gulf War because of U.S. embargo on medicines and food. He seemed surprised at the statistics and acknowledged that the embargo may well be experienced as terrorism.

He said, "I keep reminding you how much we do for other countries; now I think maybe we could do more." He reminded me that even as we spoke, Congress was passing, probably unanimously, a resolution to give the president advance authority to commit acts of retaliation without further authorization from Congress. Later he withdrew a caution ("I think you should lie low for a while") and encouraged me to keep explaining that some taxpayers, for reasons of deep belief and conscience, cannot participate in military actions.

I have learned not to attempt a conversion to my point of view, but to challenge others to live up to the highest good they know. And I expect them to return the challenge. That's the best way to teach and, more importantly, to learn.

Now is a time to talk not just of peace, but of peace and security. When desperate populations beat at our door and menace our ease of life, we have to care about reducing the repository of resentment instead of storing up more hatred. If one believes that waging war will not make U.S. citizens safer or create a more just world, then advocating for peace is an act of true patriotism, a step toward security. Addressing the needs of those most desperate aids their survival and, incidentally, our standing in the world.

Poof! Our stable reliable world is gone. Our feelings of vulnerability and fragility can be fruitful if we use this time for sustained reflection and humility. Personal self-righteousness does nothing to combat national self-righteousness.

Honesty about our own struggles is important. We were sent this useful anecdote: Following September 11, a Native American grandfather spoke to his grandson about his feelings. "I feel as if I have two wolves fighting in my heart. One wolf is the vengeful, angry, violent one. The other wolf is the loving, compassionate one." The young boy asked, "Which wolf will win the fight in your heart?" The grandfather replied, "The one I feed."

1. Michael Kelly, "Pacifist Claptrap," *The Washington Post*, 26 September 2001, p. A25.

2. Michael Kelly, "Phony Pacifists," *The Washington Post*, 3 October 2001, p. A31.

Shaken and Stirred

WINTER 2002

The United States makes people nervous. So nervous, in fact, that this January, three hundred people from twenty-nine countries gathered at the European Parliament to share their fears. Assembled were members of the European Parliament, peace workers, religious groups, relief agencies, indigenous peoples' organizations, and human rights organizations.

All shared a fearful sense that the U.S. president is declaring a U.S. right to bomb or invade any hapless country that, by his estimation, is uncooperative or sluggish in a fight he casts as "good vs. evil." The United States, they believe, has shown itself ready to unleash the most prodigious weapons of destruction against human beings and their means of livelihood. The current war is a war for revenge and resources, they say, and conclude that offense, not defense, has become the U.S. strategic posture. The president's "axis of evil" metaphor lumping Iraq, Iran, and North Korea together ignites an immense fear that a U.S. military attack on any of these states will provoke precisely the kind of catastrophe the U.S. says it wants to avoid.

In his State of the Union message the president justified an additional $48 billion for arms, bringing the U.S. total for military spending to $379 billion. Imagine the outrage. The $48 billion increase alone is more than any other country spends on its military. The total $379 billion is more than the rest of the world's combined military spending. Tragically, at the same time millions become more impoverished and die for lack of safe drinking water, food, and medicine.

The fears did not originate on September 11. There has been dismay over our president's proposal for a missile defense "star wars" system that menaces existing agreements on nuclear disarmament. European discomfort is not mitigated by the fact that, at the same time, the United States unilaterally repudiated the result of the Kyoto negotiations on environmental protection and undermined international agreements on landmines, small arms, and biological weapons.

The United Nations was formed after World War II "to save succeeding generations from the scourge of war." Yet the countries of NATO (North Atlantic Treaty Organization) make military decisions without the UN. This means that Third World countries have no voice in their actions.

Many fear a backlash from incidents in the Gulf War in which the Iraqi army, in retreat, was gunned down in what U.S. General Norman Schwarzkopf called a "turkey shoot." U.S. mine plows rolled over Iraqi trenches, plowing over anyone in them. A commander on the scene acknowledged that hundreds of Iraqis were buried alive. This is in blatant violation of the Geneva Convention, which stipulates respectful treatment for enemy dead and wounded. The dismissive U.S. response at the time: "We're not in the business of body counts." For eleven years we have bombed that country. Hundreds of thousands have died since the Gulf War because of our embargo on food and medicine. Do we think these acts will be borne without retaliation?

I attended this conference as an officer of Conscience and Peace Tax International, an organization of a number of peace tax campaigns and war tax resisters in about twenty countries. The head of the British Peace Tax Campaign and I made a presentation on conscientious objection to taxes for military force.

Throughout the conference I had a strange sense of déjà vu. It seemed like the 1980s, when the peace movement flourished. In that decade, the U.S. implanted 572 Pershing and cruise missiles on European soil. Europeans protested that the two Cold War powers, the U.S. and the Soviet Union, were putting them in the front line of combat using Europe as the football field on which they would wage a deadly nuclear war. Most of the European Peace Tax Campaigns began at that time. One even called itself the "572" after the number of missiles.

The purpose of the new European Network for Peace and Human Rights is "to take urgent steps to link up with all peoples, including especially the American peoples, whose own safety is put at risk by such a dangerous change." Linkages will be made to environmental groups (war is waste and is the greatest environmental crime), relief groups (sustainable development is impossible without peace), and human rights groups (allocation of resources that gives more to the military than to health and education prevents justice).

Already I am receiving reports that peace movements in other countries are sending representatives to be with us at the April 20 peace demonstration in Washington, D.C. Some are holding simultaneous demonstrations in their own countries that same day to show support. Human history has turned a page. Mutual fears for each other are thankfully prompting us all to action.

Forgive? Now?

"I will never understand the Taliban!" The speaker was a Muslim, addressing a panel of religious leaders. "Oh, but you must understand the Taliban," the Muslim cleric quickly replied. "It is not allowed for persons to say of others that we do not understand them. It is our human duty to understand."

Another story: Amy Biehl, a twenty-six-year-old university honors graduate and Fulbright scholar, went to South Africa to help in the struggle against apartheid. Days before she was to return to graduate school, she was driving with others outside Cape Town when four black youths pelted her car with stones, shouting the militant Pan Africanist Congress chant, "One settler [white person], one bullet!" They pulled Amy from the car, struck her in the head with a brick and stabbed her in the heart. The four were tried and convicted of the killing and sentenced.

Two years later a national healing process, the Truth and Reconciliation Commission, was set up to investigate human rights abuses by all sides during more than four decades of apartheid. Under the Government of National Unity, if they were regretful of their crime, the four could be set free.

Amy's parents, siblings, and boyfriend went to South Africa to understand the circumstances and hopelessness which engendered such hatred and revenge. Amy's murderers asked the Biehls for forgiveness. Unexpectedly, they granted it.

I spoke with Amy's parents and learned that they and their daughters' murderers now refer to each other with endearing names. Mr. Biehl said, "It is not my place to forgive. That is up to God. However, I can understand,"—there is that word again—"and I can accept."

The Biehls set up a foundation and established a youth center in South Africa to provide business backing to youth, several of whom were involved in Amy's murder. Now sports fields, skateboard parks, prisoner rehabilitation programs, literacy training, job skills instruction, childcare programs, bakeries, and parent counseling are all dedicated to empowering people who are economically and/or politically oppressed.

Observing this, Bishop Desmond Tutu exclaimed, "This senseless act of violence that would leave lesser souls embittered and vengeful unleashed a different and more powerful force. The Biehls have turned it all upside down! It is these victims in their agony who say, 'we want to help the community that produced these murderers to be transfigured.'"

Okay, but . . .

We now find ourselves in an appallingly unique time. Is it appropriate even to speak of forgiveness while an enemy gloats over those killed and shows no disposition to cease menacing our lives or to seek forgiveness? How can we leap to forgiveness while they are still intending the next round of terror?

One thing we know: the root of the problem will never be changed by punishment. Our grief and anger have the potential of developing into hatred. Vietnamese Buddhist monk Thich Nhat Hanh, reflecting on his ordeals, speaks of the need to transform raw suffering into what he calls "mindful suffering." Perhaps then we will find a way to forgiveness and compassion.

In the Palestinian/Israeli conflict, and other conflicts, one yearns for leadership's strident voices of justice on either side to acknowledge the others' suffering. Mindful suffering would mean that western nations, individually and collectively, could commit to positive long term actions to "help the communities that produced these murderers to be transfigured."

Forgiveness is not instantaneous. It does not mean excusing the behavior nor forgetting it. Here is a definition of forgiveness as outlined by Donald W. Shriver Jr., in *An Ethic for Enemies: Forgiveness in Politics* (Oxford University Press, 1995). Read it several times: "Situations of violence test our ability to demonstrate moral judgment without an instinct for revenge, an empathy for our enemies without sympathy for their crimes, and a hope that we can eventually find ways to reconcile with them."

Isn't that the only real national defense there is?

Nonviolence Is *Not* for Sissies

I'm going to give you some advice. Take it. You'll thank me. Read (or re-read) *Nonviolent Soldier of Islam: Badshah Khan, a Man to Match his Mountains* by Eknath Easwaran, (Nilgiri Press, 1999). In this time of after-shock and awe, here's an elemental education, especially for westerners who tend to equate Islam with terrorism.

Abdul Ghaffar Khan (1890-1988), a devout Muslim from the Pathan tribe, was born into wealth and privilege. His people had for centuries inhabited the rugged mountain terrain of the Khyber Pass, the British entryway into the Indian subcontinent. The early twentieth century was a time of savage British oppression.

Pathans were known as a warrior people, demanding that no wrong go unavenged. In this context, Badshah Khan seemed an unlikely candidate to develop history's first professional nonviolent army. Yet Khan persuaded his fellow Pathans to lay down their guns and fight nonviolently. Incredibly, he raised an army of one hundred thousand unarmed *Khudai Khidmatgar* (Servants of God) who united in the cause of fighting the British with passive resistance and noncooperation. He turned his people, known for their fierceness, into the largest nonviolent army this world has ever seen.

Why? How? Badshah Khan studied the Koran, fasted, and prayed. He shared his insights and called for subscribers to this oath: "I am a Servant of God; and as God needs no service, but serving his creation is serving him; I promise to serve humanity in the name of God. I promise to refrain from violence and from taking revenge. I promise to forgive those who oppress me or treat me with cruelty." Khan was upfront about the cost, calling for sacrifice, work, and forgiveness. His "soldiers" armed themselves with faith, discipline, and courage.

"There is nothing surprising in a Muslim or a Pathan like me subscribing to the creed of nonviolence," Khan insisted. "It is not a new creed. It was followed fourteen hundred years ago by the Prophet all the time he was in Mecca" (103). "Belief in God is to love one's fellow men" (55).

The price these Servants of God paid to resist the violent British occupation was immense. Hundreds were killed and many more wounded. As British troops moved in, Pathans came forward one after another to face the firing. When they fell, wounded, they were dragged back, and others came forward and exposed themselves to the fire. The corpses became so numerous that ambulances could only take them away and burn them.

Khan was repeatedly imprisoned, ultimately spending over half of his long life in prison. After a time he heard about Mohandas Gandhi and recognized in him a "great soul" who was attempting to serve God by serving the poorest of God's creation. Khan responded immediately to Gandhi's simple lifestyle and insistence upon truth and nonviolence in all of life's affairs. With great mutual respect, these two shaped the tools of nonviolence in the struggle for India's independence from Britain.

Khan once asked Gandhi how it could be that the Pathans learned nonviolence so quickly. Gandhi's immediate reply: "Nonviolence is not for cowards . . . the Pathans are more brave and courageous" (195).

This story confronts us with searching questions about the depth of our own commitment and the contemplative means by which one reaches such a dignified and loving state. We all selectively read our Scriptures. Nonviolence has a place in Christianity, Judaism, Islam, or whatever our "-ologies" or "-isms." We humans are all made of the same stuff. If they have the capacity, so do we.

Nonviolence doesn't mean that no one gets killed. It embraces a readiness to surrender one's life rather than to erase another's. That's easy for us to say and to accept philosophically. I admit that just having the correct ideas can make me feel smug and righteous. The challenge is to practice nonviolence when one is confronted with imminent threats and pain to one's self and one's family.

To quote the title of Michael True's book, nonviolence is "an energy field more intense than war."[1]

This story will make you stretch and grow, as it has done for me. I suspect our spiritual muscles will become sore, but with daily exercise they'll get strong enough. One point is clear: Nonviolence is *not* for sissies.

---

1. Michael True, *An Energy Field More Intense Than War: The Nonviolent Tradition and American Literature* (Syracuse University Press, 1995).

Listening to the Silence of Young Dead Soldiers

FALL 2003

They say: We leave you our deaths.
  Give them their meaning.
We were young, they say. We have died. Remember us.

–from "The Young Dead Soldiers," by Archibald MacLeish

In this moving poem, young soldiers killed in battle ask us to give their lives and their deaths meaning. How do we do this? How can we best honor their living and dying? First of all, we must raise our voices and do whatever we can *not* to make more young dead soldiers. We do not honor them with more deaths.

And what of the "enemy" dead, many times as many? What of the casualties who haven't seen guns or felt bombs but who are nonetheless war's victims: those who die each day for lack of food, vaccines, and medicines; those who could have benefited from money that was instead spent on military ventures? How do we give their suffering its meaning?

Regarding enemies, I admit to feeling somewhat self-righteous because I don't actually hate anyone. But that won't let any of us off the hook. Holocaust survivor Elie Wiesel observes that the opposite of love is not hate. The opposite of love is indifference.

Is indifference more comfortable than love?

To love someone takes time, thoughtfulness, energy. Ways to love must be envisioned, manufactured, tested for results, and perfected by use. The civil rights movement talked about a "science of brotherly love." Strategizing and action were needed to help others face their indifference. "Con-science" means literally "with science . . . with knowing."

Indifference does give us a rest from love's compelling demands. We observe the world's pain, but it is oh-so-tempting to distract ourselves to obliterate the memories, to quiet our fears, to calm our nerves and hush the conscience. Conscience, you know, is a perishable commodity. Use it or lose it.

There is one kind of withdrawal that is essential. It connects soul and role. For this we must go deep inside ourselves and be nourished by our highest moral/religious values. There we'll find the internal green pastures, still waters and, ah! restoration of our very souls. Love's demands then become a welcome opportunity rather than a chore.

Silence in the face of injustice is not responsible citizenship. To shatter our own and others' indifference we need to give expression to the shock and awe we so deeply feel. We need not be harsh, but we need to be vivid.

You're bashful? You feel incompetent to speak out because you say you can't turn a phrase? Nonsense! You are the world's leading expert on what your conscience demands. Your words will be the most eloquent no matter how simply stated. On Capitol Hill I am frequently told that there is nothing so compelling as words written or spoken by the "true believers."

There's a special moment to be heard now. Our government has demanded that the 104 Quaker congregations in the Philadelphia Yearly Meeting garnish the wages of an employee and turn the money over to the IRS. The employee, Priscilla Adams, has refused to pay these taxes because of a conscience against such participation in war. The Religious Society of Friends is being asked to violate not only its own principles, by serving as a collection agency for the government, but also to violate the religious convictions of an employee. In its counter suit, Philadelphia Yearly Meeting is once again asking for passage of the Religious Freedom Peace Tax Fund Bill as a solution. With this legislation in Congress we have tried honestly to reconcile the demands of conscience with the obligations of citizenship.

We will continue to plead for this accommodation as long as we hear the shrill cries of those who suffer, or the silence of young dead soldiers.

Guernica: The Cover-Up

G*uernica.* The word brings up vivid images. One is a picturesque village of northern Spain. The other is Picasso's famous antiwar painting by that name. Our Spanish hosts at the International Conference on War Tax Resistance and Peace Tax Campaigns in 1994 arranged for us to visit the village of Guernica. I have also stood before the painting in Madrid.

The village of Guernica is the cultural capital of the Basque people of northern Spain, seat of their centuries-old struggle for democratic ideals and independence. On Monday, April 26, 1937, this charming town took an undesired place in history. Monday was market day, which was always like a fair in Guernica. The streets were jammed with townspeople and peasants from the surrounding hills and countryside who crowded onto the Town Square. At four-thirty in the afternoon, the busiest hour of the week, the church bells of Santa Maria rang to sound an alarm. It was too late.

Suddenly bombers appeared overhead and released a hundred thousand pounds of highly explosive and incendiary bombs on the village, slowly and methodically pounding it to rubble. Reports say that those trying to escape were cut down by strafing machine gun fire from fighter planes. The fires that engulfed the city burned for three days. One survivor observed, "The air was alive with the cries of the wounded. Pieces of people and animals were lying everywhere."

Why this unprovoked attack? Guernica was essentially chosen for bombing practice. Hitler's burgeoning war machine needed a testing ground for a new Nazi military tactic: blanket bombing a civilian population to demoralize the enemy. Franco, Spain's military dictator, proposed Guernica, a town in his own country, as a target. The bombing by the German Luftwaffe would support Franco's Nationalist army in the Spanish civil war.

The awful news reached Pablo Picasso, who was stunned by the stark black and white photographs of the bombing. As a response he painted *Guernica*, which is so large that he had to use a ladder to reach the top of the canvas. The painting was the centerpiece for the Spanish Pavilion at the 1937 World's Fair in Paris. It depicts a hodgepodge of animal and human body parts. The twisted, writhing forms include images of a screaming mother holding a dead child, a corpse with wide-open eyes, and a gored horse.

Since 1985, a reproduction of *Guernica* has hung outside the United Nations Security Council room in New York City. That seems appropriate, since it is the UN's mandate "To save succeeding generations from the scourge of war." Why was the painting recently covered for a time?

Guernica serves as a backdrop for diplomats going in and out of the Security Council. Early last year, as Secretary of State Colin Powell presented the U.S. case for war against Iraq, this antiwar painting was covered with a blue drape. One diplomat said it would not be appropriate for the U.S. ambassador or secretary of state to speak to the press surrounded by images of women, children, and animals shouting with horror, depicting the suffering of a bombing.

Need I say more about *Guernica*'s power? Was the cover-up based on fear that *Guernica* would arouse the compassion and conscience of people and states? It would seem so. I admit it is easier to look at a blue drape than to see "the air alive with the cries of the wounded" and "pieces of people and animals everywhere." But if we are to arouse compassion and conscience, we must listen to Holocaust survivor Elie Wiesel, who says, "In the face of suffering, one has no right to turn away, not to see." Only when we see can we tell it like it is and interpret the pain in whatever way we have the gift to do.

Rapping About Plowshares and Swords

I f you knew my taste in music, you would be perplexed to learn that I led the standing ovation for a rap group rhythmically chanting with loud music. It was startling and gratifying to hear the Poetics, a rap duo from Harlem, sing "Taxes for peace, not for war. Taxes for books not for bombs. Taxes for housing not for killing." Never before has rap music been such music to my ears! I knew, in that special moment on a September Saturday afternoon at New York City's Riverside Church that our campaign had reached a point of great significance.

Why would a Harlem rap group compose a song exclusively to promote the Peace Tax Fund Bill in the U.S. Congress? Their intent was to broadcast clearly and unmistakably the connection between military spending and the growing needs they see around them. Fortunately, a radio station was recording the entire program for re-broadcast to a wide audience. This remarkable gathering, "A Forum on the Peace Tax Fund," also featured a church choir from Harlem and an informative panel discussion. The meeting was sponsored and planned by the New York City Campaign for a Peace Tax Fund, now less than a year old.

Fifty percent of African-American men in New York City are unemployed. That appalling statistic, verified in a number of studies, is reported by NYC Councilman Bill Perkins, who represents the Columbia University and Harlem areas. Problems grow worse as military spending increases. Some communities inhabited by the poor look as if bombs have already fallen. The groups in society that suffer most because of "defense" spending see their livelihoods increasingly siphoned off. Many view this economic death as silent murder. Yet, the country's military policy seems to be more of the same—much, much more.

No wonder that Councilman Perkins introduced a resolution in the NYC Council in support of the Peace Tax Fund Bill. The connection between military spending and growing hardships of citizens is clear in his "Resolution in Support of the Religious Freedom Peace Tax Fund Act." Resolution No. 367 states in part: "these advanced weapons perpetrate violence not only due to their incredible destructive powers, but also due to the devastation they cause in our communities by draining essential financial resources needed to address basic human needs. . . ."

When Councilman Perkins came to Washington, D.C., last month, he and I spoke at length with Representatives Charles Rangel and Edolphus Towns. By the end of the day, four members of Congress who represent New York City (Reps Rangel, Towns, Major Owens, and José Serrano) had signed a letter urging the NYC Council to pass the resolution of support for the Religious Freedom Peace Tax Fund Bill.

The biblical vision to turn swords into plowshares has been reversed and turned upside down. Beating swords into plowshares produces food. Beating plowshares into swords, however, pays defense contractors handsomely. Military contractors do everything within their considerable power to ensure there will always be a need for new missiles, fighter planes, tanks, ships, arms, bombs, helicopters, etc. Powerful members of Congress lard the skids.

Against those odds, we see in New York City a way to solidly grasp a handle with leverage. When citizens see the connection between books and bombs exposed, they act. Here are some suggestions to help your own community understand the connections:

- Study the NYC resolution and adapt it for your own community, town or city (available at *www.peacetaxfund.org/nyc*).

- Learn the actual cost of war to your community. A great place to start is the website of the National Priorities Project (*www.national-priorities.org*).

- Enlist the cooperation of your local council of churches, peace, and civil liberties groups.

- Hold a hearing with testimonies by those who resist paying war taxes for reasons of conscience.

- Use these efforts as a way to get your congressional delegation to support the Religious Freedom Peace Tax Fund Bill.

If you think these ideas would work for you, or if you have other ideas, please let us know.

Trumping the Numbers

'Tis the season . . . budget season, that is. The cold numbers were sent to Congress. The president is asking for a $2.5 trillion budget for the fiscal year which begins in October. There's a record deficit of $427 billion. Where do they get all that red ink?

Oh yes, and the administration's "tough" budget doesn't even include the long-term costs of the wars in Iraq and Afghanistan, or the costs of his Social Security plan. Much is off-limits for cuts. "When domestic human needs are discussed," said one congressional staffer, "there is an elephant in the room—the military budget." Why is security talked about only in military terms?

Revenues are the lowest they've been since 1959 due to tax cuts (figures adjusted for inflation). So just how is this budget supposed to work? The president says that we must be prepared to "sacrifice in a time of war." What I worry about is the involuntary sacrifice forced on so many. The heaviest load will be carried by those already most disadvantaged. There will be fewer government services and increasing disparity in wealth, incomes, and opportunities between the haves and the have-nots. The major entitlement programs—Social Security, Medicare, Medicaid, and aid to needy families—will be slashed. Sixty billion dollars is to be gouged out of Medicaid alone over the next decade.

Also making an involuntary sacrifice will be future generations who have no voice in the current debate but on whose shoulders will drop the swelling trillions of government debt. The debt will balloon even faster at the end of the president's term because of hidden price tags. Not only that, future generations will have to cope with the cumulative and foreboding degradation and depletion of our environment and natural resources.

A trump card

I was listening to staff from the Congressional Budget Office explain the budget numbers. "Remember," one said, "stories trump the numbers." It was startling, but hopeful. These folks are calling for help from the various churches and agencies to translate these cold budget numbers into stories of warm people with real faces. We should not assume members of Congress have firsthand knowledge about how the national budget affects the poor and future generations.

We should also note that members of Congress are not heartless. They will respond to ways the numbers affect real people, real families, and real future generations. These critical domestic needs are the focus of growing local support for passage of the Peace Tax Fund Bill. The New York City Council Resolution in Support of the Religious Freedom Peace Tax Fund Bill states that advanced weapons perpetrate violence not only due to their incredible destructive powers "but also due to the devastation they cause in our communities by draining essential financial resources needed to address basic human needs." Conscience is based on this side of military spending also.

There are many stories that wait to be told. People in cities large (San Francisco) and small have expressed interest in working on similar city or state resolutions. We have received a grant to do this work in Rhode Island to hold hearings with a variety of witnesses. As we learn from these experiences, we'll pass them on to you.

Stay in touch with our web site. There are many ways to tell stories: write letters to the editor of your local newspaper, hold local hearings, invite TV stations to cover stories of those in poverty, visit with your member of Congress (bring stories and faces), or write letters to members of Congress (you can send letters directly from our web site). Come on May 16 to our lobby day. Let's swap our stories with each other.

Hunger is a weapon of mass destruction. So is war. So is abuse of the environment. These are moral issues. Our mandate is to seek a remedy in tax law and to trump the numbers with our stories.

An I for an I

Michelangelo, as one story relates, visited the marble quarries to select the perfect piece from which to carve a beautiful statue. One piece was unique not only for its pristine quality but for its unusual size. If it were not for a serious flaw, one could use it to carve a statue eighteen feet tall! Other sculptors examined and rejected the stone because a deep gash penetrated to the center of the piece. When Michelangelo looked at this piece, he saw something else. He saw David. If he twisted David's hips in a certain way, he could carve a perfect statue despite the flaw. When the eighteen-foot piece was finished, awed observers asked, "How could you sculpt something so beautiful?" His answer: "David was always inside. All I did was take away what didn't belong."

According to a creation story, we were fashioned from a formless mass into perfect humans. Now, however, when you look at yourself you tend to see flaws. (If not, others may be very willing to point them out!) Bulges have developed in your character, which need to be chiseled off; places have eroded and need to be patched back. Yet, the perfect you is always, and will always remain, inside. Keeping in touch with that original keeps people from falling apart.

Getting out of shape

What gets us individuals, organizations, and nations out of shape, I believe, are the delusional assumptions named by Walter Wink in his book, *Engaging the Powers* (Fortress, 1992). On all sides of conflict, it appears, there exists an "I for an I":

- Violence is redemptive, the only language enemies understand.

- A valued end justifies the use of any means.

- Rulers and managers should be rewarded by extra privileges and greater wealth.

- Those who have military strength—who control the most advanced technology, the greatest wealth, or the largest markets—are the ones who will and should survive.

- The possession of money is a sign and proof of political and social worth.

- The production of material goods is more important then the production of healthy, normal people and of sound human relationships.

- In an organization or nation, great size is proof of its power and value.

- There is no higher value or being or power than the state.

- God is the protector and patron of the state.

- Propaganda offices and political elections tend not to focus on which party is most capable of the greater compassion, but which will be truer to the delusional assumptions (increased military budgets, more prisons, stiffer sentencing for criminals).

We have no more important task than to expose and deflate the delusional assumptions.

But what are you going to do?

I have numerous conversations on Capitol Hill as I lobby which are similar to each other. As we talk, I might ask, "Do you feel safer now because of the battle in Iraq?" The member of Congress or staff responds first with silence, then, "No, I can't say that I do." This is followed by more silence, then with a shrug, "But what are you going to do?" The military option, though admittedly possibly ineffective, is at least something to do. It's a way to assert the *I*.

How do we get back into shape?

The chisel and patching trowel are best used to dig into ourselves until we reach that quiet sacred space where our perfect selves exist. Effective outreach won't happen without in-reach. Here our worth and total capacity for love are realized. Here no discrimination exists between those worthy and unworthy, deserving and undeserving. No persons are disposable in the service of some goal. Our *I* knows this. So does the world's collective *I*. So does spiritual literature.

As we chip away over the long haul, beautiful unanticipated shapes begin to emerge. We did not anticipate a close association with other peace tax campaigns around the world, the formation of Conscience and Peace Tax International, representation at the UN in Geneva and New York, a movement to pass a resolution of support for Peace Tax legislation in the New York City Council, a state-wide effort in Rhode Island, or developing ties with Cities for Peace, the organization that coordinated nearly two hundred city council resolutions against the war in Iraq.

Mohandas Gandhi said an "eye for an eye makes the whole world blind." An "I for an I" distorts us and twists us out of shape. Like Michelangelo, we must take away what doesn't belong. With each care-fully calculated tap of the hammer on the chisel, the sculptor keeps the final image in mind.

A Hoe, Anyone?

Oops, there's a typo. When the draft of the Religious Freedom Peace Tax Fund Bill reached our office last spring (for introduction in the 109th Congress) it was supposed to say, "The Framers of the United States Constitution, recognizing free exercise of religion as an inalienable right, secured its protection . . ." Instead, it read, "The *Farmers* of the United States Constitution . . ."

That started me thinking. I know (or did know) something about farming. My children have often heard tales of my Kansas childhood. My farm chores included feeding the chickens, gathering and crating the eggs, milking the cows (by hand), gathering corn cobs and wood for the heating and cooking stoves (no electricity), working in the field driving both tractor and horses, etc. I'm not sure of the great parental wisdom of relating the experiences. Perhaps it was to forestall complaints about being asked to mow the lawn, or to boast and compare my character-building chores to the relative ease of their city childhoods. The kids, however, thought it was designed to make them feel vaguely guilty. They'd roll their eyes and chant in a we've-heard-it-all-before tone, "Yeah, Mom, we know! And you walked to school five miles every morning and home five miles every night, and it was uphill both ways!" (Well, I *did* walk nearly two miles each way.)

Farming the Constitution is an apt concept. The first U.S. citizens had experienced societies that restricted and persecuted non-conformists. The seeds were self-evident truths: "all . . . created equal . . . endowed by Creator with unalienable rights . . . life . . . liberty. . . ." The conditions were right. The seeds germinated well.

The original planters left to us the responsibility for a rich harvest. For those of us who seek legal recognition for our rights to free exercise of conscience, our cultivating tools are good communication, good preparation, and good relationships with those we hope to persuade. Farmers know you cannot force growth; swords don't work. Plowshares do. Real communication takes place when honest caring relationships are built. Replanting is sometimes necessary. Farmers don't carelessly toss good seed onto unprepared soil that is too hard and confining for seed to sprout. Loosen things up in your encounters. Explain what gives rise to your deep conviction and how that affects and directs your life. Do so in non-judgmental ways. (*My* conscience doesn't tell *you* what to do.)

There is a quality in tending your crop that enriches like fertilizer. It's the special touch you bring to the communication and relationship that is uniquely yours. Seeds need warmth. Some say that watching over things as they grow improves the land. Maybe Italian wine growers, whose special touch is broadcasting classical music to their vines, are onto something. They say it works.

Blight can damage, thwart, or ruin the crop. You see crop damage when citizens are sentenced to several years in prison because they cannot in conscience pay the military portion of their taxes. They would gladly pay if they could be assured that their money would not be used for military purposes. Yet the judge, who had other options, meted out the harshest sentence in sixty years.[1]

The original constitutional "farmers" may have understood the moral necessity of allowing people to live coherent with their deepest convictions. Certainly the best citizenship is realized in the beautiful harmony of faith, morals, and practice. Archbishop Romero observed, "We plant the seeds that one day will grow. We water seeds already planted knowing that they hold future promise." We have some chores to do.

Farmers keep faith and expectations alive. When you look at the barren frosted fields of late winter and see only the first inch-tall green blades, it's absurd to think that amber waves of grain are only a few months away. But miraculously, there they are! We don't perform miracles, but we are responsible for favorable conditions out of which they happen.

Look at the stars. Farming chores can be difficult, repetitive, and tedious. They can, however, evolve into soul-full actions if we take time to absorb a sense of majesty. "The stars tell us our place," observes Barbara Kingsolver, advising, "Never treat life or a person as less than a miracle and never give up a sense of reverence." Annie Dillard adds, "Beauty and grace perform whether or not we sense them." So we might as well look.

Farming the Constitution is worth the considerable effort, even if it's uphill both ways.

---

1. On July 1, 2005, Kevin McKee, Joe Donato, and Inge Donato were sentenced to prison terms of twenty-four, twenty-seven, and six months, respectively, for their refusal to pay taxes for military use.

Appendix A

Testimony Before New York City Council Committee on State and Federal Legislation in Support of the Religious Freedom Peace Tax Fund Bill (H.R. 2631)

Forest D. Montgomery, June 9, 2005

Mr. Chairman, my name is Forest Montgomery. I appreciate this opportunity to appear before you this afternoon. I am here at the request of Marian Franz, executive director of the National Campaign for a Peace Tax Fund. And I am here because I treasure religious freedom for all.

First, a brief word about myself. The G.I. Bill enabled me to attend the Georgetown University Law Center where I was an editor of the Law Review. After graduating in June, 1956, I went to work as a tax attorney in the IRS Chief Counsel's office. I left there in 1965 to take a position as Chief, Legal Opinion Section in the General Counsel's Office at the Treasury Department. Later I served as Counselor to the General Counsel. In 1980 I retired from public service to work primarily on religious liberty issues in the Public Affairs Office of the National Association of Evangelicals. I retired in 2000. One of my fond memories is President Reagan's famous "evil empire" speech at NAE's 1983 annual convention in Orlando, Florida. (Incidentally, I am a life-long registered Republican.)

I lay no claim to being a constitutional scholar. However, twenty years in the trenches—lobbying, testifying, filing friend-of-the-court briefs, etc.— imbued me with a familiarity with, and great respect for, the religious liberty clauses of the First Amendment. In 2001, The Freedom Forum presented me its First Amendment Outstanding Service Award for championing the cause of religious liberty for all.

My statement reflects solely my personal views. While I am an evangelical lawyer—that's not an oxymoron—I do not purport to speak for the National Association of Evangelicals. I would, however, like to note in passing that, in its Statement of Conscience Concerning World Wide Religious Persecution, NAE expressed its "deep concern for the religious freedom of fellow believers, as well as people of every faith." I welcome this opportunity to share with you my thoughts on a *genuine* issue of religious freedom. It has long been little noted, unlike the press coverage eagerly given those public moralists who, in the name of religious freedom, demagogue the Decalogue.

I greatly admire the perseverance of those wonderful people who continue to press for enactment of the Religious Freedom Peace Tax Fund Bill, although I do not share their pacifist faith. We all wish that the nations and peoples of this world would learn war no more. However, as the tragic events of September 11 sadly attest, we live in a sinful, imperfect world. Hence I believe in peace through strength. A fundamental purpose of our federal government, as the Preamble to the Constitution states, is to "provide for the common defense." Unfortunately, that purpose will remain relevant for the foreseeable future. As President John F. Kennedy said, "War will exist until that distant day when the conscientious objector enjoys the same reputation and prestige as the warrior does today."

Religious freedom is the bedrock value that animates our republic, underpins morality, and defines us as a people. Yet the pleas of our fellow Americans who are conscientiously opposed to paying taxes for military purposes have largely fallen on deaf ears. They want to pay their fair share of the tax burden, but as a matter of conscience and deep religious conviction are opposed to paying for war. What is needed is a trust fund established by law which will guarantee that their tax dollars will no longer be used for military purposes. They want no part of war, either directly as combatants, or indirectly as taxpayers. They believe both are equally immoral. I agree.

While the establishment clause prohibits government endorsement of religion, it does not bar *accommodation* of religion. And that Congress has repeatedly done. For instance:

- In 1965 Congress exempted self-employed Amish from the Social Security tax. The IRS had seized the four prize mares of an Amish farmer who refused to pay the self-employment tax on the basis of his religious belief. (The Amish "take care of their own.") Congress rightly considered this accommodation of religious belief appropriate and fair because the Amish, again as a matter of religious belief, do not accept Social Security benefits and would not be entitled to them under the law.

- In 1988 Congress also exempted Amish employers of Amish employees from the employer's share of the Social Security tax, thus legislatively overruling *United States v. Lee*, 455 US 252 (1982). The Supreme Court had accepted the government's arguments that accommodation of Amish religious belief would threaten either tax administration or the budgeting and appropriation process. Congress flatly rejected these Chicken Little arguments; the Social Security system did not suffer as a result.

- In 1984 the Church Audit Procedure Act was passed by Congress to prevent unwarranted audits of churches. The Gulf Coast Covenant Church had been charged by certain disgruntled members with private inurement. These charges were unfounded, but it took two years and $100,000 to straighten out a misunderstanding that readily could have been resolved initially in a conference with IRS representatives. (The National Association of Evangelicals was heavily involved in securing enactment of that remedial legislation.)

- In 1984 Congress addressed threatened civil disobedience by fundamentalist churches because the 1983 Social Security amendments made churches liable for the payment of the employer's share of Social Security taxes. Senator Robert Dole adopted NAE's suggested solution: Allow churches to elect whether to pay the employer's share of the Social Security tax. Since such election was voluntary, it removed the compulsion to pay the tax and allowed these churches to pay it "without taxing the collection plate" which would have "rendered to Caesar" what "belongs to God." However, to preserve the universal coverage principle of the Social Security system, if a church did elect not to pay the tax, its employees would be treated as self-employed.

- Again in 1984, Congress passed the Equal Access Act to allow student-run religious clubs in the nation's high schools. This fine law legislatively overruled lower court decisions holding that such prayer in the public schools violated the Establishment Clause. (One court even said allowing such religious clubs was "too dangerous to permit.") The Supreme Court in *Grand Rapids School District v. Ball* upheld the constitutionality of that Act, with Justice Sandra Day O'Connor observing that "There is a crucial difference between government speech endorsing religion which the Establishment Clause forbids, and private speech endorsing religion, which the Free Speech and Free Exercise Clauses protect" 473 U.S. 373, 385 (1985).

- In 1986 the Supreme Court upheld an Air Force regulation which, among other things, prohibited the wearing of a yarmulke while on duty. Congress responded quickly by enacting legislation permitting the wearing of neat and conservative religious apparel by the military while in uniform, providing it did not interfere with the performance of military duties.

These representative examples of congressional responses to the religious interests of various groups of people is by no means the whole story.

Far from it. As the Congressional Research Service has stated: "Congress has repeatedly created statutory exemptions to take account of the religious needs of various organizations. . . . The United States Code is filled with religious exemptions." (See the report for Congress, "Congressional Protection of Religious Liberty" of Louis Fisher, Congressional Research Service, p. 55 [Aug. 26, 2002].)

So how is one to account for the seeming lack of concern for our fellow Americans who oppose serving as combatants in war or paying for war with their tax dollars? I suspect that there persists a latent bias against conscientious objectors who are perceived as "refusing to fight for their country." This bias endures, despite the fact that they serve during times of war in noncombatant capacities and love their country as much as anyone else. They are not somehow "un-American." It was not always thus as the past teaches us.

In Colonial America, New Jersey was split into the Province of West New Jersey and the Province of East New Jersey. West New Jersey was the first Quaker colony in America. Another group of Quakers bought East New Jersey in 1682.

This no doubt accounts for a fascinating constitutional provision of the Province of East New Jersey. It stated that "no man that declares he cannot for conscience sake bear arms" should be forced to do so, nor "forced to contribute any money for the use of arms," but shall "bear so much in other charges, as may make up that portion in the general charge of the Province." (See the reprint in *American State Papers and Related Documents on Freedom in Religion*, 4th rev. ed., p. 59 [1949].) This essentially is what the Religious Freedom Peace Tax Fund Bill, introduced by Representative John Lewis of Georgia on May 25 with more than thirty co-sponsors, is designed to do.

And why not? Conscientious objectors in colonial times, when the very fate of a fledgling nation hung in the balance, were exempted from having to bear arms. They were also exempted in the Civil War when the fate of the Union was at stake. The relevant law today remains the Selective Service Act of 1940 which exempts conscientious objectors from bearing arms and instead provides "alternative service."

Yesterday's draft law has become virtually a dead letter in this day of all-volunteer armed forces. Today there is a pressing need for relief from the real problem: the use of conscientious objectors' tax dollars for war. As I have indicated, participating in war as a combatant or paying for war are moral equivalents. H.R. 2631 would end the present dichotomy by providing that the tax dollars of conscientious objectors can only be used for non-military purposes. If enacted, it would resolve the conflict between the legitimate government duty to "provide for the common defense" and the rights of conscience of those opposed to war by providing "alternative service" for their tax dollars. Congress, in a manner of speaking, provided "alternative service" for tax dollars when it established the Presidential Election Campaign Fund in an attempt to protect the fundamental right to vote. Rights of conscience are at least as fundamental.

When laws, as applied, threaten religious freedom, those impacted will naturally strive to change them. That is good. But it would be ennobling if men and women of good will, of whatever faith (or no faith) would lend their wholehearted support to remedial legislation because they believe in religious freedom for *all*. Anything less than that principled stand diminishes us.

If the past is prologue, a difficult road lies ahead. Thus far H.R. 2631 is primarily a Democratic initiative, although it has some Republican support. Hopefully more Republicans will sign on as co-sponsors. Needless to say, religious freedom is a traditional value and would seem an essential component of "compassionate conservatism." Moreover, Justice Antonin Scalia has said that legislative accommodation of religious belief is "desirable." (*Employment Division v. Smith*, 494 U.S. 872, 890 [1990].)

The political atmosphere on Capitol Hill is currently so poisonous it approaches outright acrimony. How refreshing it would be if there were an opportunity to lessen the tension. The Religious Freedom Peace Tax Fund Bill presents Congress with such a golden opportunity at this time to put aside differences in a bipartisan effort to enhance religious freedom. As Dr. Martin Luther King Jr. said "The time is always right to do right."

I thank you for this opportunity to speak to this important issue of religious freedom, and urge adoption of your fine resolution.

Appendix B

Chronology of Activities Relating to
Peace Tax Fund Legislation

Compiled by David R. Bassett

- **1966** Johan and Frances Eliot, and Robert and Margaret Blood, members of Ann Arbor Friends Meeting (AAFM) conscientiously oppose paying military taxes supporting the Vietnam War. They engage in war tax resistance, which is reported in the national press.

- **1968** The Bloods and the Eliots persuade Thomas Towe, a Quaker student at University of Michigan (U of M) Law School, to prepare a brief to be used as part of a bill which might be submitted to Congress, recognizing the right of conscientious objection to military taxation (COMT). (This brief, as well as the original bill, are presented as Appendix C.)

- **JUNE, 1970** Lake Erie Yearly Meeting (LEYM) (Society of Friends) at its annual meeting approves a minute to be shared with all monthly Meetings in LEYM, asking Friends to consider the implications of paying for war through their federal taxes.

- **SUMMER, 1970** The LEYM minute is presented to AAFM by its clerk, Mabel Hamm.

- **SUMMER, 1970** David Bassett, member of AAFM, hears the minute, leading him to ponder whether he and his wife Miyoko should: 1) engage in war tax resistance, 2) bring the issue of COMT into the courts, or 3) work to change U.S. tax laws so as to gain recognition of the right of COMT. The Bassetts decide to begin war tax resistance; and begin efforts to change U.S. tax laws.

- **AUTUMN, 1970** David Bassett is referred to U of M Law Professor Joseph Sax by Roger Lind, of AAFM. Bassett contacts Professor Sax, seeking advice regarding drafting appropriate legislation. Prof. Sax finds a U of M law student, Michael Hall, to work with him.

- **JANUARY, 1971** David Bassett meets with Prof. Sax and Michael Hall to begin drafting a bill based on a trust fund concept. The bill draws upon Thomas Towes' brief.

- **AUGUST, 1971** The triennial conference of the General Conference Mennonite Church passes a declaration on "The Way of Peace" which says, in part, "the levying of war taxes is another form of conscription which, along with the conscription of manpower, make war possible. We are accountable to God for the use of our financial resources and should protest the use of our taxes for the promotion and waging of war. We stand by those who feel called upon to resist the payment of that portion of taxes being used for military purposes."

- **SUMMER, 1971** The draft of the World Peace Tax Fund (WPTF) Bill is proposed to AAFM and approved.

- **SUMMER, 1971** The Ann Arbor WPTF working committee is created, to move toward introduction of the WPTF Bill in Congress.

- **SEPTEMBER, 1971** The draft of the WPTF Bill is presented to, and approved by, Ann Arbor's Interfaith Council for Peace (ICP). Two ICP members, Rev. Richard Singleton and Tom Reike, are appointed to meet with Ann Arbor WPTF working committee. The committee is also joined by U of M Law School Professor Joseph Vining.

- **AUTUMN, 1971** AAFM members make an initial visit to Washington, D.C., to seek support for introduction in Congress the WPTF Bill. Roger Lind, professor of social work at U of M, visits congressional offices. David Bassett, associate professor of internal medicine at U of M, visits Washington offices of the Mennonite Central Committee, Friends Committee on National Legislation (FCNL), Church of the Brethren, and Methodist Church.

- **JANUARY, 1972** The initial meeting of Washington-based groups interested in supporting the WPTF Bill takes place at the FCNL office.

- **FEBRUARY, 1972** The General Committee of FCNL approves the following legislative policy: "We urge provision for alternative peaceful uses of taxes paid by persons who oppose war on grounds of conscience."

- **APRIL 17, 1972** The World Peace Tax Fund Bill, H.R. 14414, is introduced for the first time in the House of Representatives. Lead sponsor Ron Dellums, D-Calif., is joined by nine co-sponsors.

- **1972** The Ann Arbor-based World Peace Tax Fund Steering Committee works in concert with a Washington, D.C.-based "Washington committee," which is staffed by FCNL employee Leah Felton.

- **MAY, 1972** The first WPTF lobbyist, Chris Brown, is hired to work in Washington, D.C.

- **MARCH 20, 1974** Some sixty people attend the first annual WPTF Visitation/Seminar in Washington, D.C.

- **1974** General Conference Mennonite Church, at its triennial meeting held in St. Catherine, Ontario, passes a resolution stating, in part, "that we educate ourselves more fully regarding the pervasive militarization of our society and express ourselves more strongly, advocating a reordering of priorities toward peacemaking; that we encourage congregations to study the World Peace Tax Fund Act (U.S.), considering the possibility of supporting it."

- **1974** The search for sponsors of the WPTF Bill leads to support from the following individuals: Noam Chomsky, Ossie Davis, Harrop Freeman, Everett Mendelsohn, Linus Pauling, J. David Singer, Albert Szent-Gyorgi, Malcolm Boyd, and E. Raymond Wilson. By 1978 this list includes Elise Boulding, Dale W. Brown, Helen Gahagan Douglas, Bishop Thomas J. Gumbleton, Milton Mayer, David McReynolds, Richard McSorley S.J., Holly Near, Steven S. Schwarzschild, Ronald J. Sider, John M. Swomley Jr., Mary Luke Tobin S.L., George Wald, Jim Wallis, Dr. Cynthia C. Wedel, and John Howard Yoder.

- **1974** The search begins for organizational sponsors of the WPTF Bill. Early organizational sponsors include five Quaker Yearly Meetings: New York, Baltimore, Philadelphia, Illinois, and Iowa Friends (Conservative). By 2008, this list includes 198 organizations.

- **1974** Michio Ohno, a Japanese Mennonite in Tokyo, reports to David Bassett that he and other Mennonites in Japan "are starting a movement to get WPTF legislation in Japan."

- **MARCH 13, 1975** Ron Dellums introduces the WPTF Bill (H.R. 4897) in the House of Representatives for the second time. He is joined by eighteen co-sponsors.

- **APRIL 4, 1975** The Ann Arbor and Washington WPTF offices merge and are renamed the National Council for a World Peace Tax Fund (NCWPTF). Board leadership includes David Bassett, chair; Delton Franz, director of the Mennonite Central Committee Washington Office, vice-chair; Ralph Smeltzer, director of the Church of the Brethren Washington Office, treasurer. Strong ties exist from the outset with Brethren,

Mennonite, Quaker, Presbyterian, and Methodist denominations. Early staff and board members largely come from these denominations.

• **APRIL, 1975** Washington, D.C., office of NCWPTF opens at 2121 Decatur Place, NW, with three part-time staff: Program Coordinator Bill Samuel, Office Administrator Leah Felton, and Congressional Liaison Chris Brown. Friends Meeting of Washington provides office space, beginning a relationship between NCWPTF and the Friends Meeting of Washington which continues to this day.

• **1975–1982** NCWPTF office is coordinated by Bill Samuel (Quaker), followed by Sister Mary Rae Waller, O.P., (Catholic), followed by Bill Strong (Quaker).

• **JUNE, 1975** The first World Peace Tax Fund Newsletter (Vol. II, No. 3) is published from the new NCWPTF office.

• **MARCH 19, 1976** Congress holds its first hearing on the World Peace Tax Fund Bill, H.R. 4897, in the House of Representatives Ways and Means Committee. The hearing is chaired by James A. Burke, D-Mass.

• **MAY, 1976** The General Conference of the ten million-member United Methodist Church endorses the following resolution: "We, therefore, support all those who conscientiously object: to preparation for or participation in any specific war or all wars; to cooperation with military conscription; or to the payment of taxes for military purposes; and we ask that they be granted legal recognition."

• **APRIL, 1977** Senator Mark Hatfield, R-Ore., introduces the World Peace Tax Fund Bill (S. 880) in the Senate.

• **1977–1979** Delton Franz serves as NCWPTF board chair. Subsequent board chairs are Alan Eccleston, 1980–1982; Robert Hull, 1982–1988; Edie Gause, 1989; Ben Richmond, 1990–1994; Bill Galvin, 1995–2001 and 2008–present; Steve Ratzlaff, 2001–2008; and J.E. McNeil, 2008.

• **APRIL, 1978** More than sixty people attend the fourth annual Washington, D.C., Seminar/Visitation.

• **MAY, 1978** NCWPTF produces a slideshow and study guide called "Conscience & War Taxes."

• **1978** New Call to Peacemaking Conference issues statement in support of WPTF Bill.

- **1979** General Conference Mennonite Church passes a resolution establishing the Historic Peace Church Task Force on Taxes and endorsing a three-year effort in support of the WPTF Bill.

- **JANUARY, 1981** NCWPTF creates a network of volunteers in various congressional districts around the U.S. Initially, forty-two people join this network of "Congressional District Contacts."

- **1981** Historic Peace Church Task Force on Taxes publishes *Affirm Life: Pay for Peace; A Handbook for World Peace Tax Fund Educators/Organizers*.

- **1982** General Conference Mennonite Church sends a delegation to the IRS.

- **FEBRUARY 23, 1982** U.S. Supreme Court rules against Lee in *U.S. v. Lee*. In this case, Lee, an Amish employer of Amish employees, sought exemption from paying tax for Social Security, since the Amish do not accept Social Security benefits. Lee's claim was based on the First Amendment right to free exercise of religion. The Supreme Court decision included the following wording: "Because the broad public interest in maintaining a sound tax system is of such a high order, religious belief in conflict with the payment of taxes affords no basis for resisting the tax." As Edward Snyder states in his chapter (beginning on page 40), this and other Supreme Court decisions reinforce "the need to petition Congress to recognize conscientious objectors' refusal to pay for war."

- **MARCH 16–18, 1982** Lead sponsor Ron Dellums convenes ad hoc congressional hearings on the WPTF Bill. WPTF Program Coordinator Bill Strong testifies: "The IRS cannot provide the religious pacifist with any form of administrative relief. The courts have repeatedly offered no judicial recourse. So that segment of our society that would live as conscientious objectors and peacemakers must seek legislative relief from Congress in the form of the World Peace Tax Fund Bill."

- **SEPTEMBER, 1982** Robert Hull becomes chair of the NCWPTF board of directors and editor of *God & Caesar* newsletter, a publication of the General Conference Mennonite Church.

- **SEPTEMBER, 1982** Marian Franz becomes executive director of the NCWPTF.

- **1983** Congressional district contacts now number 103, in 41 states.

- **1983** National Council for a World Peace Tax Fund changes its name to "National Campaign for a Peace Tax Fund" (NCPTF).

- **1983** NCPTF newsletter begins to report on international peace tax fund efforts in New Zealand, United Kingdom, and West Germany.

- **OCTOBER 1984** Philadelphia Quakers form the Friends Committee on War Tax Concerns, which aims to address the issues of war tax refusal, "corporate conscience," and corporate response to individual actions in regard to war tax refusal.

- **1985** NCPTF approves changing the name of the World Peace Tax Fund Bill to the "U.S. Peace Tax Fund Bill." This change comes in response to awareness that peace tax organizations in other nations are uncomfortable with the use of "world" in the bill's name.

- **1985** NCPTF considers whether to include a component of war tax resistance in its work. The board of directors decides to focus specifically on legislative work, but to be in relationship with other organizations whose focus is war tax resistance, referring persons inquiring about war tax resistance to those organizations.

- **SEPTEMBER, 1985** The Peace Tax Foundation is incorporated as an *educational* organization to compliment the *legislative* work of NCPTF. (NCPTF maintains passage of the U.S. Peace Tax Fund Bill as its primary goal.)

- **1986** The first International Conference on War Tax Resistance and Peace Tax Campaigns is held in Tübingen, West Germany. Marian Franz and David Bassett attend as representatives of NCPTF.

- **1986** The U.S. Peace Tax Fund Bill is co-sponsored by fifty-five representatives in the Ninety-Ninth Congress, its largest number of sponsors to date.

- **1988** The Friends Committee on War Tax Concerns publishes *Handbook on Military Taxes & Conscience.* The book is sponsored by Friends World Committee for Consultation (1506 Race Street, Philadelphia, Pa. 19102).

- **1988** NCPTF testifies in the House Ways and Means Committee Subcommittee on IRS, focusing on the "frivolous return" penalty, which had been added to the Tax Equity and Fiscal Responsibility Act of 1982 (TEFRA). The testimony states that "enactment of a legislative accommodation, such as the U.S. Peace Tax Fund Act—analogous to the conscientious objector provision of the Selective Service law and no more problematic than existing provision for certain objectors to the Social Security system—would alleviate a persistent burden on the IRS while permitting these few but undeterrable citizens to pay their full share of tax without violation of religious conscience."

• OCTOBER, 1988 An important legal precedent, relevant to the Peace Tax Fund Bill is passed. The Technical Amendments and Miscellaneous Revenue Act of 1988 (TAMRA) reinstates an "exemption from Social Security, granted to employers and employees who are both members of certain religious faiths."

• 1988 The Legislative Advisory Group is created, comprised of five or six staff persons from Washington-based advocacy organizations, to work with and advise Marian Franz.

• 1990 *Peace and Taxes . . . God and Country,* by Chel Avery, is published by the War Tax Concerns Support Committee of the Philadelphia Yearly Meeting of Friends (1515 Cherry St., Philadelphia, Pa. 19102).

• AUGUST 3–5, 1990 Bryn Mawr College hosts "Celebration of Conscience," attended by almost four hundred persons from many states and several countries. Parren Mitchell, former member of Congress and co-sponsor of the U.S. Peace Tax Fund Bill, delivers the keynote address.

• 1991 Marian Franz helps found the Faith and Politics Institute, a non-partisan interfaith organization which seeks to help public officials stay in touch with their faith and deeper values as they shape public policy.

• APRIL 17, 1991 The U.S. Peace Tax Fund Bill is introduced in the House of Representatives by its new lead sponsor, Andy Jacobs, D-Ind.

• 1991 The Peace Tax Foundation publishes *Communities of Conscience: Collected Statements on Conscience and Taxes for Military Preparations,* edited by Bernd G. Janzen.

• 1991 The NCPTF publishes *Speaking for Conscience: A Manual for Peace Tax Fund Activists,* by Edith Gause.

• 1991 Marian Franz completes *Questions That Refuse to Go Away: Peace and Justice in North America,* which is published by Herald Press, Scottdale, Pa.

- **1991** The Quaker Council on European Affairs in Brussels, Belgium, publishes *Paying for Peace: Lobbying for Legislation*.

- **MAY 21, 1992** Congress holds a hearing on the U.S. Peace Tax Fund Bill, H.R. 1870, in the Subcommittee on Select Revenue Measures of the House Ways and Means Committee. Charles Rangel, D-N.Y., chairs the hearing, which includes oral testimony from more than twenty-five persons (including several members of Congress), written statements by over one hundred persons, and letters of support from more than twenty-five hundred persons from all fifty states. The hearing is covered in many national newspapers. (See *Congressional Record*, Serial 102-98, pp. 1-295.)

- **1992** The second edition of *Communities of Conscience: Collected Statements on Conscience and Taxes for Military Preparations*, edited by Linda Coffin, is published by The Peace Tax Foundation.

- **1992** Conscience and Peace Tax International (CPTI) is founded at the fourth International Conference on War Tax Resistance and Peace Tax Campaigns in Brussels, Belgium. Marian Franz is involved in the formation of CPTI, an organization that works through international movements and institutions such as the United Nations and the European Union to obtain full legal recognition of conscientious objection to paying for armaments and war. CPTI asserts that no human being should be compelled to participate in military violence, directly or indirectly (*www.cpti.ws*).

- **APRIL, 1994** NCPTF files, from David & Miyoko Bassett's home, are donated to U of M's Bentley Historical Library, at 1150 Beal Avenue, Ann Arbor, Michigan. (Accepted as Papers, 1963–1994 from donor number 8242, the collection is open for research.)

- **1994** CPTI articles of incorporation are adopted at the fifth International Conference on War Tax Resistance and Peace Tax Campaigns in Hondarribia, Spain.

- **1996** CPTI is incorporated by Belgian Royal Decree, making CPTI eligible to apply for Non-Governmental Organization (NGO) status in the United Nations.

- **JANUARY, 1997** The Peace Tax Foundation receives 501(c)(3) non-profit status from the Internal Revenue Service as an educational organization.

(NCPTF continues as a 501(c)(4) advocacy organization which cannot receive tax-deductible contributions due to its lobbying work.)

- **MAY, 1998** NCPTF board members hold a retreat to discuss history of the campaign, successes achieved, and steps needed in the future.

- **JUNE 11, 1999** CPTI is granted "special consultative status" as an NGO in the Economic and Social Council of the UN. This status confers rights to attend and make written and oral contributions to certain UN meetings, especially those concerned with human rights.

- **1999** Marjorie E. Kornhauser publishes "For God and Country: Taxing Conscience" in the *Wisconsin Law Review* Vol. 1999, No. 5: 940-1016.

- **1998** The U.S. Peace Tax Fund Bill name is changed to the "Religious Freedom Peace Tax Fund Bill" (RFPTF Bill), to emphasize its importance in relation to the First Amendment right to freedom of religious expression. The RFPTF Bill's lead congressional sponsor becomes Representative John Lewis, D-Ga., an ardent civil rights advocate and coworker with Martin Luther King, Jr.

- **2000** Emily Miles writes *A Conscientious Objector's Guide to the UN Human Rights System*, published by the Quaker United Nations Office, Geneva, and CONCODOC (Conscription and Conscientious Objection Documentation); 5 Caledonian Rd., London N1 9DX, England.

- **MAY 22–26, 2000** The Millennium Forum takes place at the UN Headquarters in New York City. NCPTF board members David Bassett, John Randall, and Rosa Packard attend to lobby on behalf of COMT. They achieve partial success, having included, in the Forum's final statement, the following words: "Further, in the context of the right not to be complicit in killings, we call for full legal recognition of the rights of conscientious objectors." (This text is found in section D 8, dealing with human rights, of *Peoples' Millennium Forum; Declaration and Agenda for Action; Strengthening the UN for the Twenty-First Century*.)

- **JULY, 2000** Eighth International Conference on War Tax Resistance and Peace Tax Campaigns takes place at Catholic University in Washington, D.C. The conference is jointly organized by NCPTF and the National War Tax Resistance Coordinating Committee.

- **2005** Derek Brett writes *Military Recruitment and Conscientious Objection: A Thematic Global Survey*, published by CPTI.

- **APRIL, 2005** CPTI representatives Marian Franz, Rosa Packard, and Derek Brett travel to Geneva, Switzerland, to give testimony on COMT before the UN Commission on Human Rights.

- **JUNE 9, 2005** New York City Council holds a hearing on Resolution No. 367, in support of the Religious Freedom Peace Tax Fund Act, H.R. 2631. The lead sponsor in City Council is Councilmember Bill Perkins.

- **OCTOBER 20, 2005** Following a four-month campaign in Rhode Island, the Providence City Council votes unanimously for a resolution supporting the RFPTF Bill, making Providence the first city in the U.S. to pass such a resolution.

- **DECEMBER 5, 2005** Rhode Island State House holds a public hearing on the RFPTF Bill in Providence, R.I.

- **DECEMBER, 2005** Marian Franz retires after twenty-three years as executive director of NCPTF, with plans to continue lobbying part-time for the RFPTF Bill. These plans never materialize due to illness.

- **JANUARY–MAY, 2006** Tim Godshall serves as interim executive director of NCPTF

- **2006** *Conscience and the Courts: Selected Supreme Court and other cases which define conscientious objection to participation in war*, by Marian Franz, is published by the Peace Tax Foundation.

- **JUNE 1, 2006** Alan Gamble becomes executive director of NCPTF

- **NOVEMBER 17, 2006** Marian Franz dies after a struggle with cancer.

- **FEBRUARY 17, 2007** A memorial service is held for Marian Franz at her church, Hyattsville, Md., Mennonite Church. Preceded in death by her husband, Delton, on March 6, 2006, and by her siblings, Vernon Claassen and Doris Claassen, she is survived by her three children, Gregory, Gayle, and Coretta; two grandchildren; and two sisters, Edith Graber and Joanne Claassen.

- **2007** Peace Tax Foundation releases DVD *Compelled by Conscience*, an informational video about the need for a Peace Tax Fund.

- **JUNE–NOVEMBER, 2008** Melani Hom serves as interim executive director of NCPTF.

- **NOVEMBER 10, 2008** Bethany Criss becomes executive director of NCPTF.

The 1972 World Peace Tax Fund Bill as Introduced in the Ninety-Second Congress

WORLD PEACE TAX FUND ACT

HON. RONALD V. DELLUMS
OF CALIFORNIA

IN THE HOUSE OF REPRESENTATIVES
Monday, April 17, 1972

Mr. DELLUMS. Mr. Speaker, today is the deadline for the filing of income tax returns in the United States. My colleague from New York (Mr. ROSENTHAL) and I, along with eight of our colleagues, are taking this opportunity to introduce legislation which we believe is essential to the integrity of this Nation's tax system.

The World Peace Tax Fund Act, as our bill is called, would amend the Internal Revenue Code to establish conscientious objector status for taxpayers identical to that established presently under our Selective Service laws. Under this act, any man or woman in the country who felt he or she could not, in good conscience, contribute to military expenditures would have the option of having their tax dollars routed instead to peace-related activities.

It has long been recognized in this body and throughout the Nation that thousands, perhaps millions, of our citizens are so strongly compelled to resist violence that participation in war in any form is morally and religiously intolerable. What our laws have not yet recognized is that many of these citizens are equally opposed to seeing their tax dollars spent on implements of death and destruction.

The World Peace Tax Fund Act recognizes this moral conviction and, without lowering anyone's total tax bill, removes the great dilemma now facing conscientious objectors—to disobey their own beliefs or to disobey the laws of their country.

The original authors of this measure are to be highly praised for their contribution to this crucial effort. Among those responsible for the drafting of this legislation were David R. Bassett, M.D., of Ann Arbor, Mich.; Joseph L. Sax and G. Joseph Vining, members of the University of Michigan Law

School faculty; Michael P. Hall, a law student there; and Richard Sandler.

Joining Mr. ROSENTHAL and me in sponsoring this bill are Mr. KASTENMEIER, Mr. RANGEL, Mrs. ABZUG, Mr. BINGHAM, Mr. CONYERS, Mr. DIGGS, Mr. MITCHELL, and Mr. RYAN.

At this time I would like to insert into the RECORD a summary of the legislation, followed by the text of the bill and other related material:

SUMMARY

The World Peace Tax Fund Act proposes that the Internal Revenue Code of 1954 be amended to provide an alternative to contribution to military spending for Federal taxpayers who are conscientiously opposed to participation in war, and that a Fund be established to receive and distribute to qualified peace-related activities the portion of such individuals' tax payments that would otherwise go to military spending. The remainder of qualifying individuals' income, estate, and gift taxes would be transferred to the general fund of the U.S. Treasury, to be spent only for non-military purposes.

The Act gives relief to those citizens conscientiously opposed to participation in war, who are presently forced to violate their beliefs by participating in war through tax payments. There is considerable precedent for such relief. The Selective Service System has long recognized and accommodated the beliefs of conscientious objectors. Tax exemptions have been provided for certain religious groups to avoid violation of their religious and conscientious beliefs.

The requested tax relief for conscientious objectors will not open the "floodgates" to similar relief for other groups. The conscientious objector's request for tax relief is exceptionally compelling because it is motivated by the widely held and long-established fundamental religious and moral mandate—"Thou shalt not kill."

The Act provides taxpayers, who are conscientiously opposed to war and who might otherwise feel compelled to undertake illegal tax resistance, with a means of making a meaningful contribution to world peace consistent with their obligations of citizenship. It is particularly important that the Act extends the opportunity for conscientious objection to women and to men not eligible for conscientious objector status under the Selective Service System.

The amendments to the Internal Revenue Code of 1954 provide that a qualified taxpayer may elect to have his or her Federal income, estate, or gift tax payment transferred to a special trust fund, the World Peace Tax Fund. The amendments also explain how a taxpayer qualifies to have his or her tax paid to the Fund. Other sections of the Act provide for the creation of the World Peace Tax Fund, and for the appointment of a Board of eleven Trustees to administer the Fund. The Fund is modeled after the National Highway Trust Fund and the National Airport and Airway Trust Fund. The Act provides that the General Accounting Office shall annually determine and publish the percentage of the Budget of the United States which was spent for military purposes in the fiscal year just ended. This percentage will be used to determine the portion of the qualifying taxpayer's tax which shall be received by the Board; the Board shall submit a budget to Congress for approval and appropriation, providing for channeling of these monies to specified peace-related activities. Monies not appropriated from the Fund for expenditures budgeted by the Board shall remain available for use in subsequent years by the Board, subject to Congressional appropriation.

H.R. 14414

A bill to amend the Internal Revenue Code of 1954 to provide that a taxpayer conscientiously opposed to participation in war may elect to have his income, estate, or gift tax payments spent for non-military purposes; to create a Trust Fund (the World Peace Tax Fund) to receive these tax payments; to establish a World Peace Tax Fund Board of Trustees; and for other purposes.

Be it enacted by the Senate and House of Representatives of the United States of America in Congress assembled, that this Act may be cited as the "World Peace Tax Fund Act."

SEC. 2. WORLD PEACE TAX FUND.

(a) OPERATION OF TRUST FUND.—There is hereby established within the Treasury of the United States a special trust fund to be known as the "World Peace Tax Fund" (hereinafter referred to as the "Fund"). The Fund shall consist of such amounts as may be transferred to the Fund as provided in this section.

(b) TRANSFER TO FUND OF AMOUNTS EQUIVALENT TO CERTAIN TAXES.—

(1) IN GENERAL.—There is hereby transferred to the Fund amounts equivalent to the sum of the amounts designated during the fiscal year by individuals under Section 6099 of the Internal Revenue Code of

1954 for payment into the Fund, and amounts during the fiscal year as estate tax payments designated for payment into the Fund under section 2210 of such Code, and amounts received during the year as gift tax payments designated for payment into the Fund under section 2505 of such Code. Such amounts shall be deposited into the Fund, and shall be available only for the purposes provided in section 8 of this Act.

(2) METHOD OF TRANSFER.—The amounts transferred by paragraph (1) shall be transferred at least monthly from the general fund of the Treasury to the Fund on the basis of estimates by the Secretary of the Treasury of the amounts, referred to in paragraph (1), received in the Treasury. Proper adjustments shall be made in the amounts subsequently transferred to the extent that prior estimates were in excess of or less than the amounts required to be transferred.

SEC. 3. INCOME TAX PAYMENTS TO WORLD PEACE TAX FUND.

(a) Subchapter A of Chapter 61 of the Internal Revenue Code of 1954 (relating to returns and records) is amended by adding at the end thereof the following new part:

"PART IX—DESIGNATION OF INCOME TAX PAYMENTS FOR TRANSFER TO WORLD PEACE TAX FUND.

"SEC. 6098. QUALIFICATION FOR PARTICIPATION IN THE FUND.

"(1) Any taxpayer who has actually qualified as a conscientious objector for Selective Service or Immigration purposes shall be entitled to participate in the Fund.

"(2) Any taxpayer not covered by Subsection 1 of this section, who declares that he or she is conscientiously opposed to participation in war, within the meaning of the Military Selective Service Act, as amended, shall qualify to designate payment of his or her income taxes to the Fund, as provided in Sec. 6099.

"(a) Qualification for participation in the Fund shall be demonstrated by an affirmative response to the following question, which shall appear on all personal income, estate, and gift tax forms: 'Do you believe that you are conscientiously opposed to participation in war, within the meaning of the Military Selective Service Act as amended?'

"(b) Instructions provided to taxpayers by the Secretary to help them in filing tax returns shall include an explanation of the purpose of the Fund; the essential features of the Military Selective Service Act, as amended, pertaining to conscientious objection to war.

"(3) Persons shall acquire the status of conscientious objector by their affirmative declaration to the question specified in paragraph (2a) above, provided, however, that the Secretary may initiate an action in the U.S. District Court of the district in which the declaring taxpayer has his residence, to challenge his status as a conscientious objector.

"Sec. 6099. DESIGNATION BY INDIVIDUALS.

"(a) IN GENERAL.—Every individual (other than a nonresident alien) whose income tax liability for any taxable year is $1 or more may designate that his income tax payment for that year shall be paid into the World Peace Tax Fund established by section 2 of the World Peace Tax Fund Act.

"(b) DEFINITIONS.—As used in this section—

"(1) INCOME TAX LIABILITY.—The term "income tax liability" means the amount of the tax imposed by chapter 1 on an individual for any taxable year (as shown on his return) reduced by the sum of the credits (as shown on his return) allowable under section 33 (relating to foreign tax credit), section 35 (relating to retirement income), section 38 (relating to certain depreciable property), section 40 (relating to work incentive program credit), and section 41 (relating to political contributions).

"(2) INCOME TAX PAYMENT.—The term "income tax payment" means the amount of taxes imposed by chapter 1 paid by or withheld from an individual for any taxable year not in excess of his income tax liability.

"(c) MANNER AND TIME OF DESIGNATION.—A designation under subsection (a) may be made with respect to any taxable year.

"(1) at the time of filing the return of the tax imposed by chapter 1 for such taxable year, and

"(2) at any other time (after the time of filing the return of the tax imposed by chapter 1 for such taxable year) specified in regulations prescribed by the Secretary or his delegate."

(b) (1) The table of contents of such Code is amended by inserting after the item relating to part VIII of subchapter A of Chapter 61 the following:

"PART IX. DESIGNATION OF INCOME TAX PAYMENTS
FOR TRANSFER TO WORLD PEACE TAX FUND."

(2) The table of contents of subtitle F of such Code is amended by

inserting after the item relating to section 6096 the following:

"PART IX. DESIGNATION OF INCOME TAX PAYMENTS FOR TRANSFER TO WORLD PEACE TAX FUND.
"SEC. 6099. DESIGNATION BY INDIVIDUALS."

(3) The table of parts of subchapter A of chapter 61 of such Code is amended by adding at the end thereof the following:

"PART IX. DESIGNATION OF INCOME TAX PAYMENTS FOR TRANSFER TO WORLD PEACE TAX FUND."

(c) The amendments made by this section shall apply with respect to taxable years beginning after December 31, 1971.

SEC. 4. ESTATE TAX PAYMENTS TO WORLD PEACE TAX FUND.

(a) Subchapter C of Chapter 11 of the Internal Revenue Code of 1964 is amended by adding at the end thereof the following new section:

"SEC. 2210. DESIGNATION OF ESTATE TAX PAYMENTS FOR TRANSFER TO WORLD PEACE TAX FUND.

"(a) IN GENERAL.—An individual may elect that the tax imposed by section 2001 on his taxable estate shall be transferred when paid to the World Peace Tax Fund established under section 2 of the World Peace Tax Fund Act."

(b) The table of contents for subchapter C of Chapter 11 of such Code is amended by adding at the end thereof the following:

"SEC. 2210. DESIGNATION OF ESTATE TAX PAYMENTS FOR TRANSFER TO WORLD PEACE TAX FUND."

(c) The amendments made by this section shall apply with respect to taxable years beginning after December 31, 1971.

SEC. 5. GIFT TAX PAYMENTS TO WORLD PEACE TAX FUND.

(a) Subchapter B of Chapter 12 of the Internal Revenue Code of 1954 is amended by adding at the end thereof the following new section:

"SEC. 2505. DESIGNATION OF GIFT TAX PAYMENTS FOR TRANSFER TO WORLD PEACE TAX FUND.

"(a) IN GENERAL.—An individual may elect that the tax imposed by section 2501 shall be transferred when paid to the World Peace Tax Fund established under section 2 of the World Peace Tax Fund Act."

(b) The table of contents for subchapter B of Chapter 12 of each Code is

amended by adding at the end thereof the following:
"SEC. 2505. DESIGNATION OF GIFT TAX PAYMENTS FOR TRANSFER TO WORLD PEACE TAX FUND."

(c) The amendments made by this section shall apply with respect to taxable years beginning after December 31, 1971.

SEC. 6. AUTHORIZATION OF APPROPRIATIONS.

(a) As soon after the close of each fiscal year as may be practicable, the Comptroller General shall determine and certify to the Congress and to the President the percentage of all expenditures made by the United States during the preceding fiscal year which were made for a military purpose (see "Definitions," below). The certification shall be published in the Congressional Record upon receipt by the Congress.

(b) There is hereby authorized to be appropriated each year a certain portion of the Fund to the World Peace Tax Fund Board of Trustees (established by Sec. 7) for obligation and expenditure in accordance with the provisions of this Act. This portion is determined by applying the percentage figure derived in subsection (a) above to the monies transferred to the Fund in each fiscal year, and adding to that sum all monies in the Fund previously authorized to be appropriated to the Board of Trustees but not yet appropriated. Monies remaining in the Fund shall accrue interest according to the prevailing rate in long-term government bonds.

(c) The remaining portion of the Fund is authorized to be appropriated to the general fund of the Treasury of the United States. No part of the money transferred to the general fund under this subsection shall be appropriated for any expenditures, or otherwise obligated for military purposes.

SEC. 7. BOARD OF TRUSTEES.

(a) There is established a World Peace Tax Fund Board of Trustees (hereinafter referred to as the "Board") which shall be composed of 11 members appointed as follows:

(1) nine members (not more than five from the same political party, appointed by the President, by and with the advice and consent of the Senate, from among individuals who have demonstrated a consistent commitment to world peace and international friendship and who have had experience with the peaceful resolution of international conflict; and

(2) two members, who shall also meet the above criteria, one of whom shall be appointed by the President pro tempore of the Senate from among the Members of the Senate, and one of whom shall be appointed by the Speaker of the House of Representatives from among the Members of the House. Members appointed under this paragraph shall serve ex officio.

(b) The term of office of each member of the Board shall be six years except that the term of office for four of the members initially appointed under subsection (a) (1) shall be three years. Members may serve until their successors are appointed, except that if any member appointed under subsection (a) (2) ceases to serve as a member of Congress, his term of office on the Board shall terminate at the time he ceases to serve as a Member of Congress. Each member shall be eligible for reappointment for one additional term, but no person shall serve for more than 12 years as a member of the Board. Six Trustees shall constitute a quorum.

(c) Any vacancy in the membership of the Board shall not affect its powers and shall be filled in the same manner in which the original appointment was made. The term of office of any person appointed to fulfill the unexpired term of a member shall consist of the unexpired portion of such member's term.

(d) The Board shall elect a Chairman from among its members.

SEC. 8. DUTIES OF THE BOARD.

(a.) The Board may make payments as authorized by Appropriation Acts, by way of grant, loan, or other arrangement, under such conditions and upon such terms as it considers necessary.

(b) Funds designated for the purpose of research may be directed to governmental or nongovernmental, national or international organizations. Funds for non-domestic programs involving the providing of goods and services shall be restricted in distribution to the United Nations and associated agencies.

(c) Activities eligible to receive money from the Board shall include but not be limited to:

(1) Research directed toward developing and evaluating non-military and nonviolent solutions to international conflict;

(2) Disarmament efforts;

(3) International exchanges for peaceful purposes;

(4) Improvement of international health, education, and welfare; and

(5) Programs for providing information to the public about the above activities.

(d) The Board shall publish regulations for the submission of applications for funds by persons and agencies, and shall determine the eligibility of such persons and agencies to receive payments or loans. Before approving the application of any such person or agency the Board shall determine, after a comprehensive review of all the functions and activities of the person or agency requesting approval, that such functions and activities have a non-military purpose.

(e) The Board shall submit its budget to Congress as stipulated in Sec. 9, shall report to the President and to the Congress annually on its activities, and shall provide a complete accounting of all funds received and disbursed pursuant to this Act.

(f) It is the intent of this Act that the Fund shall not operate to release money for military expenditures which, were it not for the existence of the Fund, would otherwise have been appropriated for non-military expenditures.

SEC. 9. SUBMISSION OF BUDGET.

Notwithstanding any other provision of law, the Comptroller General shall carry out the activities and review of the Board which would be carried out by the Office of Management and Budget if the Board were an agency within the executive branch of the Government; and may establish such requirements as he deems necessary to carry out his authority under this section. The Office of Management and Budget shall not have Jurisdiction over the Board. The Board shall submit its budget, requests for appropriations and related reports to the Congress in accordance with such requirements and procedures as the Comptroller General may establish.

SEC. 10. POWERS AND ADMINISTRATIVE PROVISIONS.

(a) Each department, agency, and instrumentality of the Federal Government, including independent agencies, is authorized and directed to cooperate with and furnish to the Board, to the extent permitted by law, upon request made by the Chairman, such information as the Board may require to fulfill its duties under this Act.

(b) Subject to such regulations as the Board may adopt, the Chairman may—

(1) appoint and fix the compensation of an Executive Director and such additional staff personnel as he deems necessary; and

(2) procure temporary and intermittent services to the same extent as authorized by section 3109 of title 5, United States Code.

(c) Members of the Board shall be compensated at the maximum rate permitted by law for government employees or consultants, on a per diem basis, and shall be reimbursed for travel, subsistence, and other necessary expenses incurred in the performance of their duties as members of the Board.

SEC. 11. AMNESTY.

(a) Any individual who incurs or has incurred a civil or criminal penalty for failing or refusing to pay all or a part of the tax imposed on him by chapter 1 of the Internal Revenue Code of 1964 (relating to income tax) for any taxable period with respect to which the time for filing a claim for credit or refund of overpayment has not expired on the date of enactment of this Act is granted amnesty if he—

(1) pays any tax due (with interest) which he failed or refused to pay (on the grounds set forth in paragraph (2) (A)), and

(2) establishes, to the satisfaction of the Secretary of the Treasury, that—

(A) his failure or refusal to pay was on the grounds that all or a part of his tax payment would be used by the United States for carrying out military activities, and

(B) he would have made timely payment of such tax and designated his tax payment for payment into the World Peace Tax Fund (established under section 2 of this Act) if this Act had been in effect at the time of his failure or refusal to pay the tax.

(b) Whenever any individual is granted amnesty under subsection (a), the Secretary of the Treasury shall transfer to the World Peace Tax Fund the amount of any tax payment made under subsection (a) by such individual, and remit to that individual the amount of any civil penalty (other than interest) for which amnesty was granted.

SEC. 12. DEFINITIONS.

For the purposes of this act—

(1) "Military purpose" means any activity or program conducted, administered, or sponsored by an agency of the Government which effects an augmentation of military forces, defensive and offensive intelligence activities, or enhances the capability of any person or nation to wage war, and "Expenditures for a military purpose" includes but is not limited to amounts expended by the United States in connection with—

(A) the Department of Defense;

(B) the Central Intelligence Agency;

(C) the National Security Council;

(D) the Selective Service System;

(E) activities of the Atomic Energy Commission that have a military purpose;

(F) activities of the National Aeronautics and Space Administration that have a military purpose;

(G) foreign military aid, and foreign economic aid made available to any country for the purpose of releasing local funds for military activities; and

(H) the training, supplying, or maintaining of military personnel, or the manufacture, construction, maintenance, or development of military weapons, installations, or strategies;

(2) "agency" means each authority of the Government of the United States, whether or not it is within or subject to review by another agency, but does not include—

(A) the Congress; or

(B) the courts of the United States; and

(3) "person" includes an individual, partnership, corporation, association, or public or private organization other than an agency.

SEC. 13. SEPARABILITY.

If any section, subsection, or other provision of this Act or the application thereof to any person or circumstance is held invalid, the remainder of this Act and the application of such section, subsection, or other provision to other persons or circumstances shall not be affected thereby.

MEMORANDUM IN SUPPORT OF THE WORLD PEACE TAX FUND ACT

Many persons in this country are conscientiously opposed to participation of any kind of nature in war. For some religious denominations this is a fundamental part of the religious beliefs of the members. For example, the Handbook of the Pacific Yearly Meeting of the Religious Society of Friends urges its members:

"To recognize that the military system is not consistent with Christ's example of redemptive love ... [and] to consider carefully the implication of paying those taxes, a major portion of which goes for military purposes."—page 28 of 1962 Revised Edition.

The World Peace Tax Fund Act is designed to relieve individuals conscientiously opposed to participation in war from the obligation to participate in war through the payment of taxes for military spending. Also it frees them from the weight of conscience which comes from breaking the law, when they hold law and society important.

Freedom of conscience, whatever that conscience might be, is an integral part of our scheme of government. The Supreme Court of the United States, in March 1965, quoted a statement made in 1919 by Harlan Fiske Stone, who later became Chief Justice of the Court:

> Both morals and sound policy require that the state should not violate the conscience of the individual. All our history gives confirmation to the view that liberty of conscience has a moral and social value which makes it worthy of preservation at the hands of the state. So deep is its significance and vital, indeed, is it to the integrity of man's moral and spiritual nature that nothing short of the self-preservation of the state should warrant its violation; and it may well be questioned whether the state which preserves its life by a settled policy of violation of the conscience of the individual will not in fact ultimately lose it by the process (Stone, The Conscientious Objector, 21 Col. U.Q. 253, 269 [1919]).

Although not all persons who are conscientiously opposed to participation of any kind in war base their convictions on religious training and belief, conscientious objection to war appears to be well recognized as an integral part of the religious beliefs of many people. Speaking of the struggle for religious liberty in this country, Chief Justice Hughes referred to:

The large number of citizens of our country, from the very beginning, who have been unwilling to sacrifice their religious convictions, and in particular, those who have been conscientiously opposed to war and who would not yield what they sincerely believed to be their allegiance to the will of God (*United States v. Macintosh*, 283 U.S. 605, 631 [1931]).

Certainly to require significant participation in war, against the religious conscience of these people, would violate the spirit of the first amendment protection for the free exercise of religion. (See *West Virginia State Board of Education v. Barnett*, 319 U.S., 624 (1943); *School District of Abington Township v. Schempp*, 374 U.S. 203 (1963); *Contran, Tyrell v. United States*, 200 F. 2d 8 (9th Cir. 1953), *cert. denied* 345 U.S. 910.)

Conscientious objection to war and military training is deeply imbedded in the traditions of this country. For example, the ratifying conventions of each of the six states that recommended the adoption of a Bill of Rights in ratifying the new Constitution approved specific amendments as a part of their recommendation; Virginia, North Carolina, and Rhode Island included a provision guaranteeing the right of conscientious objection. (See Elliot, *Debates on the Adoption of the Federal Constitution*, Vol. 3, p. 659, Vol. 4, p. 244, Vol. 1. p. 334-36 (reprint of second ed. 1937).

A similar provision was suggested but rejected by the Maryland convention. (See Elliot as 553.) It is not surprising, therefore, that one of James Madison's proposed amendments presented to the first session of the first Congress included the following language: "but no person religiously scrupulous of bearing arms shall be compelled to render military service in person" (*Annals of the Congress of the United States*, 434 [Gales and Seaton, 1934]).

During the debates on the proposed amendment, it was suggested that the right be conditioned "upon paying an equivalent." To this suggestion Mr. Sherman of Connecticut remarked:

"It is well known that those who are religiously scrupulous of bearing arms are equally scrupulous of getting substitutes or paying an equivalent. Many of them would rather die than do either one or the other" (*Annals* at 750).

A motion was then made to drop this clause altogether; the motion failed and the clause was included in the list of proposed amendments sent to the Senate for approval. The Senate omitted this provision and it never became a part of our Bill of Rights. Although no record of the Senate debates was taken at the time, the opposition to the proposal in the House would indicate that the Senate preferred to leave the matter to legislation instead of a Constitutional Amendment (*Annals* at 751).

Although Congress has recognized the right of conscientious objectors to refrain from participation in war and has enacted legislation to protect that right, conscientious objectors are still forced to participate in war through the payment of taxes, a substantial portion of which goes to military spending. Every person in this country who pays Federal income, estate, or gift taxes is forced to participate in war in this manner. They are forced to aid in the equipping and training of armies and in the purchase of bombs, ammunition, missiles, napalm and other instruments of destruction. This is a significant form of participation in war.

Tax refusal—refusal to pay taxes because the money was to be spent for things to which the taxpayers were conscientiously opposed—has a long history. Early Christians refused to pay taxes to Caesar's pagan temple in Rome. Quakers and Mennonites refused to pay taxes to pay for the war effort during the French and Indian Wars, the Revolutionary War, and the Civil War. Under Gandhi's influence, strugglers for independence in India refused to pay taxes to the British Empire. In many ways the Boston Tea Party and other attempts of the colonists to prevent the British from collecting taxes to pay for the French and Indian War and for the stationing of British troops in the colonies represent similar protests (See Malone & Rauch, *Empire for Liberty* 126-36 [1960]). Just as pacifists are opposed as a matter of conscience to paying taxes that are used for military purposes, so were the colonists opposed as a matter of conscience to paying taxes without representation.

At the present time those who are conscientiously opposed to any form of participation in war can avoid violating their conscience in the matter of Federal income taxation in only two ways. First, they can carefully avoid earning more than the minimum income required by Federal law upon which income taxes must be paid. Second, they can simply refuse to pay the taxes due, or a certain percentage of them; this amounts to a criminal offense which could result in a maximum sentence of $10,000 fine and one year in prison. (See Internal Revenue Code, Section 6502.) Such a penalty could conceivably be imposed every year if the individual refused to pay the taxes due every year. Despite the possibility of these extreme consequences, many people take this route because they feel it is a lesser evil than to violate their conscience.

To most American citizens who wish to make substantial contribution to the life of their community and who want to be law-abiding citizens these are not feasible alternatives. The liberty of conscience that Chief Justice Stone spoke about is not being preserved in the area of conscientious opposition to participation in war. To preserve this liberty of conscience and to preserve both the dignity and the fairness of law—to preserve it in a spirit intended by the founding fathers and the drafters of the Bill of Rights—legislation should be enacted to provide a legal and realistic alternative to participation in war through the payment of federal income, estate, and gift taxes.

PRECEDENT

There is sound precedent for such legislation giving tax relief to protect religious and conscientious beliefs. Section 1402(e) of the Internal Revenue Code provides an exemption from payment of self-employment taxes for duly ordained, licensed or commissioned ministers and members of religious orders, or for Christian Science practitioners upon their filing an application for exemption together with a statement that they are conscientiously opposed to, or because of religious principles, they are opposed to participation in an insurance plan like that provided by the Social Security Act. Section 1402(h) of the Internal Revenue Code similarly relieves members of qualified religious faiths, primarily the Amish, of the duty to pay the Social Security tax. By this Code provision, enacted in 1965, Congress acknowledged and accommodated the conscientious objection of the Amish to participation in insurance plans. The tax exemptions provided by sections 1402(e) and 1402(h) of the Internal Revenue Code were modeled after the exemption of conscientious objectors from the draft.

By exempting individuals conscientiously opposed to participation in insurance plans from payment of Social Security taxes, Congress clearly extended the principle of Congressional accommodation of conscientious beliefs from the area of the draft to the area of taxation. Thus Congressional precedent for tax relief to accommodate the beliefs of conscientious objectors to war is firmly established. Congress has recognized both the right not to participate in war and the right of a tax exemption to avoid participation in a program to which the tax-payer is conscientiously opposed.

The proposed tax accommodation for conscientious objectors to war recognizes the unique and long-acknowledged right of an individual to refrain from participation in war. It reflects an honest acknowledgment that payment of taxes for military spending is a significant and, for conscientious objectors, intolerable form of participation in war. The proposed special tax status for conscientious objectors is a necessary device to avoid forcing their participation in war.

The tax treatment asked for conscientious objectors is less exceptional than that presently granted by sections 1402(e) and 1402(h) of the Internal Revenue Code. Those sections allow individuals "conscientiously opposed" to Social Security insurance to be entirely exempted from payment of a portion of their tax. In contrast, the World Peace Tax Fund Act does not propose exemptions from payment of a portion of the conscientious objector's tax. Under the Act, a conscientious objector is still required to pay his entire tax. The Act merely provides that an appropriate portion of the tax may be diverted from military spending to non-military peace-related activities.

Like the exemption from payment of the Social Security tax, the proposed tax accommodation for conscientious objectors is based on religious and conscientious belief. The conscientious objector to war has a compelling justification for the special tax status he seeks. His concern is fundamental. He asks not to be forced to join in the deliberate killing of his fellow men. His desire not to participate in war and killing through any means, including taxation, is based upon a widely acknowledged religious and moral principle. Observance of the principle is essential to the integrity of the individual. By forcing the conscientious objector to war to contribute to military spending, Congress presently forces him to violate his conscience and severely denies his right of religious freedom.

The tax accommodation of conscientious objectors would be an affirmative gesture which would benefit society as well as the individual taxpayer. Especially today, when a faint hope of world peace precariously counterbalances the threat of unspeakably destructive war, it is important to society that the moral principle, "Thou shalt not kill," which underlies the conscientious objector's attitude toward war, be firmly and repeatedly asserted.

Fundamental fairness requires that the opportunity for making this affirmative gesture for world peace and against killing be extended to all people—not just those draft-age males who quality for conscientious objector status under the Selective Service laws. Therefore another important aspect of this act is that it offers women and children an opportunity constructively to demonstrate their opposition to war through formal conscientious objection—an opportunity which at present is open only to draft-age men.

The proposed tax accommodation for conscientious objectors is required by uniquely compelling justifications. Granting this special tax status to conscientious objectors will not open the floodgates to other groups who claim to be "conscientiously opposed" to various uses of their tax dollars, because the concern of the conscientious objector is so fundamental, so widely acknowledged, and so essential to the integrity of individuals and our society.

The contemplated tax treatment of conscientious objectors does not establish a precedent for individual earmarking of tax dollars. Trustees appointed by the President with the advice and consent of the Senate will receive, for subsequent channeling to appropriate peace-related activities, a portion of the Fund's monies. This portion represents the sum of all qualifying individuals' income, estate, or gift tax payments, multiplied by the percentage of last year's Federal budget devoted to military spending. The spending decisions of the Trustees require Congressional approval and appropriation. Congress retains power over spending of the conscientious objector's taxes. The taxpayer who qualifies as a conscientious objector can only decide that his tax dollars will not be spent for one specific purpose—military spending. Distribution of monies by the Board to qualified peace-related organizations finds precedent in the qualified distribution requirements for private foundations under Section 4942 of the Code.

In summary, the conscientious objector's uniqueness rests first, in the long tradition of Congressional respect for and accommodation of conscientious objectors to war. Second, the standards for determination of conscientious objector status have been tried, proven, and refined by the Selective Service System and conveniently provide stringent and reliable requirements for determining conscientious objector status for tax purposes. Third, the conscientious objector to war bases his request for special tax treatment on a widely held, long-established, fundamental religious and moral belief. Fourth, the declaration of conscientious objection for tax purposes is an affirmative and constructive act which could make a substantial contribution to world peace.

The great interest of individuals in the free exercise of their fundamental religious beliefs should weigh most heavily against the public interest in minimizing exceptions to the general tax laws. If the interest of the Amish in not participating in Social Security insurance was sufficient to outweigh this public interest, the compelling interest of the conscientious objector to war should also outweigh it.

EFFECTIVENESS

Individuals conscientiously opposed to war will be excused from tax contribution to military spending and thereby from a significant form of participation in war. The tax dollars diverted from military spending will be used to promote world peace. It is recognized that because of the nation's tax collection and budgeting process, the creation of the World Peace Tax Fund may not markedly reduce the money available for military spending. A serious curtailment of military spending would result only if a great many taxpayers participated in the Fund, thereby calling for a major shift in national priorities. The military will get the funding it requests until the success of the Fund helps persuade taxpayers and Congress to reduce the priority of military spending.

At present, many conscientious objectors are so determined to change this country's priorities that they have refused to pay their taxes. As an alternative to forcing conscientious objectors to pursue this difficult and unpopular course, this bill offers the conscientious objector a way of making a positive contribution to world peace in place of contributing to military spending. The Fund will provide a constructive means of citizen's protest for its contributors. The Fund will draw the attention of every tax-payer to the percentage of American tax dollars going to military spending. It will encourage Congress to recognize this percentage by publication of the Fund's annual reports. At present, for the most part, no effort is being made by the government to separate military spending from other spend-ing. Individual taxpayers, in making out their annual returns, will be forced to decide whether or not they can conscientiously contribute to military spending. Those who become conscientious objectors for tax purposes will be voicing a significant vote against military policy. The bill provides that the number of contributors to the Fund, the amount of money contrib-uted, and the expenditures of the Fund shall be published and reported to Congress each year.

Many conscientious objectors would like to take a firmer stand than that provided by this Act in opposition to their country's military opera-tions, but in view of the political constraints imposed on them as a minority, they support the Fund as a meaningful, though not entirely satisfactory, means of working for world peace.

The Internal Revenue Code amendments and the organization of the Fund are designed to accomplish their goals with a minimum of admin-istrative effort. The individual taxpayer is given the initial responsibility for determining whether he or she is eligible for conscientious objector status. A taxpayer who is already classified as a conscientious objector for Selective Service or Immigration purposes is automatically eligible. A tax-payer, regardless of age or sex, who files a declaration of conscientious opposition to war, is eligible. False statements knowingly made in declar-ing conscientious objector status are grounds for prosecution for perjury. Willful abuse of this claim of eligibility will therefore be discouraged. The Internal Revenue Service may conduct an examination, "For the purpose of ascertaining the correctness of any return," according to Section 7602 of the Code. Language in that section is broad enough to allow review of a declaration of conscientious objection to war. In formulating requirements for conscientious objector status and in reviewing returns of conscientious objectors, it is expected that the Secretary or his delegate will rely primarily on 50 U.S.C. App. 456(j), which exempts conscientious objectors from military service, and judicial interpretations thereof. Final rulings by the IRS against the taxpayer's status as a conscientious objector are appealable to the United States District Court.

The Fund itself will be self-sufficient. It is expected that the commitment of the Fund's Trustees to world peace and their appointment by the President with the advice and consent of the Senate will make the Fund self-policing so that contributors and other taxpayers and Congress will have faith in it, and it will accomplish the goals set for it. The operating expenses of the Fund will be paid out of the money the Fund receives from taxpayers. Because the Fund will encourage people who presently refuse to pay their taxes to pay these taxes, the administrative costs of the Fund will be offset by the additional tax payments which the Fund is expected to generate.

A final point is that legislative relief is the only legal avenue available for resolving the conscientious objector's dilemma between his beliefs and his obligations of citizenship. Conscientious objectors have repeatedly lost their battle against war taxes in the courts. Despite the strong constitutional arguments which can be made in their defense, in deference to Congress the courts have repeatedly held against conscientious objectors who have refused to pay their taxes to military spending.

CONSTITUTIONALITY

(1) Uniformity

The proposed legislation conforms with the requirement of Article I, Section 8, Clause 1 of the Constitution which provides "All duties, imports and excises shall be uniform throughout the United States." The requirement of uniformity has been read to require geographical uniformity (*Knowlton v. Moore*, 178 U.S. 41 (1900); *Brushaber v. Union Pacific Rail Co.* 240 U.S. 1 (1916); *Fernandez v. Wiener*, 326 U.S. 340 [1945]).

(2) First Amendment

The First Amendment provides "Congress shall make no law respecting the establishment of religion, or prohibiting the free exercise thereof." The proposed tax payment accommodation of the religious beliefs of conscientious objectors is a mitigation of a general requirement for the purpose of allowing the free exercise of religion. This is not an establishment of religion.

According to the General Counsel of the Treasury, "The classic example of the application of the free exercise clause is the series of cases which have upheld Congressional exemption of conscientious objectors from military service. The validity of this exemption was first established by the Selective Draft Law Cases, 245 U.S. 366 (1918), upholding the exemption in the draft law of members of religious sects whose tenets prohibited the man's right to engage in war." The Solicitor General had argued (p. 374) that the exemption did not establish such religions but simply aided their free exercise. The court considered that the congressional authority to provide such exemption was so obvious that it need not argue the point (pp. 389-390).

The present Universal Military Training and Service Act (50 U.S.C. app. 456. (j)) provides, "(j) Nothing contained in this title (sections 451, 453, 454, 455, 456, and 458-471 of this Appendix) shall be construed to require any person to be subject to combatant training and service in the Armed Forces of the United States who, by reason of religious training and belief, is conscientiously opposed to participation in war in any form." "Participation in war in any form" has been read by the courts to mean "participation in any form in war" (*Taffs v. U.S.*, 208 F. 2d 329 (Ca. 8 [1953], *cert. denied* 347 U.S. 928 [1954]). In *U.S. v. Seeger* (380 U.S. 163, 13 L. Ed. 2d 733 [1965]) the court broadly interpreted "by reason of religious training and belief" to require no formal religious training, and suggested that a personal moral code would be sufficient grounds for conscientious objection if there were some other basis for the registrant's belief. The *Seeger* case did not reach the constitutional question of whether the state might require a belief in God as a condition for exemption. *Torcaso v. Watkins* (367 U.S. 488 [1961]) did hold that Maryland could not require an oath attesting to a belief in God as a requirement for becoming a notary public, because such a requirement would constitute an establishment of religion.

Another example of the use of Congressional authority to make exemptions from general laws to permit the free exercise of religion is the exemption from taxation of religious organizations, property and activities. These exemptions continue to be upheld against claims that they have the effect of establishing the religions benefited (*Swallow v. U.S.*, 325 F. 2d 97 [Tenth Cir. 1963]).

Zorach v. Clauson (343 U.S. 306 [1952]) is another case affirming the validity of accommodations made by the state to allow the free exercise of religion. There the Court upheld New York legislation authorizing public schools to release children one hour early every week for religious instruction off school grounds.

That allowing conscientious objectors to pay a portion of their taxes into a non-military tax fund is an accommodation for the free exercise and not an establishment of religion is made clear by *Sherbert v. Verner* (374 U.S.

398 [1963]). The Court held there that Maryland could not deny unemployment benefits to a Seventh-Day Adventist who refused to take a job requiring work on Saturday, the Adventists' Sabbath. The Court held this conditioning of welfare benefits on compromise of individuals' religious beliefs was an unconstitutional restriction on the free exercise of religion. Therefore, the Court ordered Maryland to make accommodation within its general unemployment law.

A conscientious objector who is forced to pay taxes which help finance military spending is being denied the right of free exercise of his religious beliefs. The conscientious objector's plight is worse than the Adventist's in *Sherbert* who paid a lesser price for free exercise of religion. In *Sherbert*, the price exacted by the state for religious freedom was loss of unemployment benefits. The conscientious objector who refuses to pay taxes is not only fined but is forced to break the law and is liable to criminal prosecution. Contribution to military spending is a significant form of participation in war. It may be as offensive to religious beliefs as service in the Armed Forces. Congress has accommodated religious beliefs by exempting from military service those conscientiously opposed to participation in war. It is a small step for Congress to allow the conscientious objector not to participate in war through taxes. Clearly, such an accommodation is to aid the free exercise of religion and is permitted, if not required, by the First Amendment.

The effect of the proposed accommodation for conscientious objectors would not be discrimination in favor of some religions at the expense of others. Rather, the present discrimination against those who are forced to pay taxes (a portion of which goes to military spending in violation of their religious beliefs), would be removed (see *Sherbert*, p. 406). Nor are the problems of administration and the possibility of spurious claims under the proposed accommodation justification for continuing the present burdens on the free exercise of religion (see *Sherbert*, p. 407).

Despite the constitutionality of the proposed amendments, it might be argued there is an overriding public interest which forbids accommodation. But in *In Re Jenison* (375 U.S. 14 [1963]) the Court relying on *Sherbert v. Verner* vacated a ruling of the Minnesota Supreme Court, which held that jury duty, a primary duty of all citizens, was superior to a religious belief which forbade judging others and therefore forbade jury duty. After *Jenison* it is possible to argue that it is unnecessary to balance the public interest against the individuals' interest to determine whether an exception to the general law should be made to accommodate the free exercise of religion. Rather Congress or the courts could simply determine if an accommodation is necessary to allow free exercise of religion and, if so, grant it.

(3) Due Process Clause

The due process clause of the Fifth Amendment requires that tax statutes be reasonable and apply to a reasonable class. However, the standards of reasonableness applied to tax statutes are more lenient than those applied generally; only clearly arbitrary tax classifications will be struck down (*Fleming v. Nestor*, 363 U.S. 603 [1960]; *Smart v. U.S.*, 222 F. Supp. 65 [1963]; *Leeson v. Celebrezze*, 225 F. Supp. 527 [1963]). Therefore it is unlikely that the classification proposed by these amendments would be found unreasonable, especially since the classification is the same which has long been accepted as reasonable for draft exemption purposes.

The 2007 Religious Freedom Peace Tax Fund Bill as Introduced in the One Hundred Tenth Congress

RELIGIOUS FREEDOM PEACE TAX FUND ACT
H. R. 1921

To affirm the religious freedom of taxpayers who are conscientiously opposed to participation in war, to provide that the income, estate, or gift tax payments of such taxpayers be used for nonmilitary purposes, to create the Religious Freedom Peace Tax Fund to receive such tax payments, to improve revenue collection, and for other purposes.

IN THE HOUSE OF REPRESENTATIVES
April 18, 2007

Mr. LEWIS of Georgia (for himself, Mr. CONYERS, Mr. MCGOVERN, Mr. FARR, Mr. MCDERMOTT, Mr. PAUL, Ms. CARSON, Mr. CLAY, Mr. ELLISON, Mr. FATTAH, Mr. HINCHEY, Ms. EDDIE BERNICE JOHNSON of Texas, Mr. KUCINICH, Ms. NORTON, Mr. OBERSTAR, Mr. SERRANO, and Ms. WOOLSEY) introduced the following bill; which was referred to the Committee on Ways and Means

A BILL

To affirm the religious freedom of taxpayers who are conscientiously opposed to participation in war, to provide that the income, estate, or gift tax payments of such taxpayers be used for nonmilitary purposes, to create the Religious Freedom Peace Tax Fund to receive such tax payments, to improve revenue collection, and for other purposes.

Be it enacted by the Senate and House of Representatives of the United States of America in Congress assembled,

SECTION 1. SHORT TITLE.

This Act may be cited as the 'Religious Freedom Peace Tax Fund Act'.

SEC. 2. FINDINGS.

Congress finds the following:

(1) The free exercise of religion is an inalienable right, protected by the First Amendment of the United States Constitution.

(2) Congress reaffirmed this right in the Religious Freedom Restoration Act of 1993, as amended in 1998, which prohibits the Federal Government from imposing a substantial burden on the free exercise of religion unless it demonstrates that a compelling government interest is achieved by the least restrictive means.

(3) Many people immigrated to America (including members of the Quaker, Mennonite, and Church of the Brethren faiths) to escape persecution for their refusal to participate in warfare, yet during the First World War hundreds of conscientious objectors were imprisoned in America for their beliefs. Some died while incarcerated as a result of mistreatment.

(4) During the Second World War, "alternative civilian service" was established in lieu of military service, by the Selective Training and Service Act of 1940, to accommodate a wide spectrum of religious beliefs and practices. Subsequent case law also has expanded these exemptions, and has described this policy as one of " . . . long standing tradition in this country . . ." affording 'the important value of reconciling individuality of belief with practical exigencies whenever possible. It dates back to colonial times and has been perpetuated in state and federal conscription statutes,' and 'has roots deeply embedded in history' (*Welsh v. United States,* 1970, Justice Harlan concurring). During and since the Second World War thousands of conscientious objectors provided essential staff for mental hospitals and volunteered as human test subjects for arduous medical experiments, and provided other service for the national health, safety and interest.

(5) Conscientious objectors have sought alternative service for their tax payments since that time. They request legal relief from government seizure of their homes, livestock, automobiles, and other property; and from having bank accounts attached, wages garnished, fines imposed, and imprisonment threatened, to compel them to violate their personal and religious convictions.

(6) Conscientious objection to participation in war in any form based upon moral, ethical, or religious beliefs is recognized in Federal law, with provision for alternative service; but no such provision exists for taxpayers who are conscientious objectors and who are compelled to participate in war through the payment of taxes to support military activities.

(7) The Joint Committee on Taxation has certified that a tax trust fund , providing for conscientious objector taxpayers to pay their full taxes for non-military purposes, would increase Federal revenues.

SEC. 3. DEFINITIONS.

(a) Designated Conscientious Objector—For purposes of this Act, the term "designated conscientious objector" means a taxpayer who is opposed to participation in war in any form based upon the taxpayer's sincerely held moral, ethical, or religious beliefs or training (within the meaning of the Military Selective Service Act (50 U.S.C. App. 456(j)), and who has certified these beliefs in writing to the Secretary of the Treasury in such form and manner as the Secretary provides.

(b) Military Purpose—For purposes of this Act, the term 'military purpose' means any activity or program which any agency of the Government conducts, administers, or sponsors and which effects an augmentation of military forces or of defensive and offensive intelligence activities, or enhances the capability of any person or nation to wage war, including the appropriation of funds by the United States for—

(1) the Department of Defense;

(2) the intelligence community (as defined in section 3(4) of the National Security Act of 1947 (50 U.S.C. 104a(4));

(3) the Selective Service System;

(4) activities of the Department of Energy that have a military purpose;

(5) activities of the National Aeronautics and Space Administration that have a military purpose;

(6) foreign military aid; and

(7) the training, supplying, or maintaining of military personnel, or the manufacture, construction, maintenance, or development of military weapons, installations, or strategies.

SEC. 4. RELIGIOUS FREEDOM PEACE TAX FUND.

(a) Establishment—The Secretary of the Treasury shall establish an account in the Treasury of the United States to be known as the 'Religious Freedom Peace Tax Fund' for the deposit of income, gift, and estate taxes paid by or on behalf of taxpayers who are designated conscientious objectors. The method of deposit shall be prescribed by the Secretary of the Treasury in a manner that minimizes the cost to the Treasury and does not impose an undue burden on such taxpayers.

(b) Use of Religious Freedom Peace Tax Fund—Monies deposited in the Religious Freedom Peace Tax Fund shall be allocated annually to any appropriation not for a military purpose.

(c) Report—The Secretary of the Treasury shall report to the Committees on Appropriations of the House of Representatives and the Senate each year on the total amount transferred into the Religious Freedom Peace Tax Fund during the preceding fiscal year and the purposes for which such amount was allocated in such preceding fiscal year. Such report shall be printed in the Congressional Record upon receipt by the Committees. The privacy of individuals using the Fund shall be protected.

(d) Sense of Congress—It is the sense of Congress that any increase in revenue to the Treasury resulting from the creation of the Religious Freedom Peace Tax Fund shall be allocated in a manner consistent with the purposes of the Fund.

www.ingramcontent.com/pod-product-compliance
Lightning Source LLC
Chambersburg PA
CBHW031508270326
41930CB00006B/314